RADICAL ISLAM IN AMERICA

RADICAL ISLAM IN *AMERICA*

Salafism's Journey from Arabia to the West

CHRIS HEFFELFINGER

FOREWORD BY DAVID COOK

Potomac Books, Inc.
Washington, D.C.

Library of Congress Cataloging-in-Publication Data
Heffelfinger, Christopher.
  Radical islam in america : salafism's journey from arabia to the west /
Chris Heffelfinger ; foreword by David Cook. — 1st ed.
      p. cm.
  Includes bibliographical references and index.
  ISBN 978-1-59797-302-1 (hardcover : alk. paper)
  1. Islamic fundamentalism—United States. 2. Muslims—Political
activity—United States. 3. Salafiyah—United States. I. Title.
  BP67.U6H44 2011
  320.5'570973—dc22

                                    2010049193

Potomac Books, Inc.
22841 Quicksilver Drive
Dulles, Virginia 20166

First Edition

10 9 8 7 6 5 4 3 2 1

Contents

Foreword

SALAFI-JIHADISM, the most visible and violent form of radical Islam at the present time, has its intellectual, religious, and social roots in both pre-modern Islam as well as the exigencies of the contemporary world. There is little consensus among students of salafism or the broader phenomenon of "radical Islam" as to how to define these terms, and with that lack of consensus comes the knowledge that the people represented by them reject any description that would differentiate them from the much larger mass of Muslims.

Radical Islam is a tendency that can be traced back approximately one hundred years and has a number of commonalities that bind it together. Dominant among these commonalities is a radical reformist treatment of the state of Islam as a whole, and most specifically the rejection of Sufism (the most common medium through which Muslims have practiced Islam for the past 1,000 years) as a form of polytheism. Radicals see most especially the intermediaries by which Sufis reach the divine (usually holy men either living or deceased) as being nothing other than *shirk* (associating other beings with God, the primal sin in Islam), and reject the spiritual structures Sufis have built up around these intermediaries (shrines, veneration of graves, etc.) as being essentially a continuation of paganism within Islam.

If radical Islam only focused upon Sufism it would be revolutionary enough, but its radicalism is manifested by a wide range of reforms that aim to take away the Sufi primacy within the world of Islam. These include an intense scripturalist focus upon the Qur'an (as opposed to the tradition literature or *hadith*) as well as a tendency to reject the traditional legal schools of Sunni Islam, adopting an eclectic legal philosophy, and a determination to implement the *Shari'a* (divine law) in its totality throughout the Muslim world. Other elements include a willingness to absorb Western technological and scientific advances into the Muslim world (anathema to conservative Muslims), to integrate women into positions of influence in their groups, to use technological media such as the Internet to spread their message, and a missionary fervor to convert both other Muslims as well as non-Muslims to their cause.

Radical Islam in this broad social sense has religious, social, and intellectual implications for the world of Islam. Religiously speaking, it confronts the conservative world of the *'ulama'* (learned class), and seeks to aggressively place Islam within the modern world. Socially it represents a revolutionary movement that appeals hugely to marginal and nonpious cultural Muslims, especially within the university setting, and especially within the disciplines of the hard sciences. For most outsiders radical Islam socially is a conservative force, because it emphasizes elements of Islam such as gender segregation and dress code that place it in opposition to liberal Western values. Intellectually, it is quite eclectic, and can embrace both a triumphalistic reading of Islamic history as one that is leading to a messianic caliphal state as well as a conspiracy-theory-based-idea that non-Muslims are trying to annihilate all Muslims.

It is from this last intellectual point that Salafi-jihadism becomes so important within the world of radical Islam. Salafism was originally a term used by such reformers as Muhammad 'Abdu (d. 1905), meaning "following the pious ancestors," who tended to integrate Western liberal traditions into classical Islam and were also hostile toward Sufism. But by the 1960s under the influence of Muhammad Qutb (brother to the more famous Sayyid Qutb, leader of the Muslim Brethren in Egypt) the term was adopted by radicals who both rejected Sufism and Western liberalism, as well as the conservative tendencies of the mainstream *'ulama.* Not all Salafis are jihadis it is important to note. Many withdraw from society to form their own counter-societies, or engage in missionary works or private piety in order to fulfill the requirements of their faith.

Salafi-jihadis, on the other hand, take an activist approach to the question of establishing a Muslim state (as they hold that all contemporary Muslim states are tainted by their association with Western non-Muslim governments or their unwillingness to implement the *Shari'a* in its totality). They see the medium of jihad or divinely sanctioned warfare as being central in both confronting non-Muslim powers and in the redemption of Muslims and their salvation. It is this focus upon jihad as a salvific and necessary force that places Salafi-jihadis in such stark opposition to all other Muslims. Traditionally while jihad was a part of Islam, it was never a dominant part, let alone a criterion by which one decided who was a good Muslim or not. Salafi-jihadis have made jihad into the most important facet of Islam, and concentrate upon it in a single-minded manner that differentiates them from most other Muslims.

This single-minded concentration can take many forms, both in terms of religious and intellectual reframing of Islam as a whole as well as the formation of groups and organizations designed to practice jihad against Muslim enemies (in order to form a Muslim state) as well as non-Muslim enemies (who are judged to be either oppressing Muslims or occupying territory deemed to historically have belonged to Muslims). Salafi-jihadis intellectually have revived the discussion of jihad, largely dormant since medieval times, and contributed significantly to theological-political debates concerning the legitimacy of fighting, types of possible targets and tactics as well as the promotion of a vast cult of martyrdom current throughout the Internet (either through literary documentation or on-line videos). From a practical point of view, Salafi-jihadis view the fact that they are "defending Islam" as one that confers upon them spiritual authority that otherwise would belong exclusively to the *`ulama'*. It is for this reason that structurally Salafi-jihadis are to a large extent the enemies of the *`ulama'*—ultimately they seek to replace their authority based upon learning with the authority of the fighter defending Islam.

Chris Heffelfinger's work on the contemporary ramifications of Salafi-jihadism, especially those in the United States, is an important and succinct summary and exposé of a dangerous and growing phenomenon. He documents the origins of Salafism, its originally reformist agenda, and its later development into radicalism and amalgamation (to a large degree) with the Saudi Arabian variety of Wahhabism. Throughout the course of ten fast-paced chapters, he takes the reader through a wide range of material, documenting the ideological links of Salafis with mainstream Muslims, including those prominent in the American Muslim community today, as well as the murky world of Muslim charities, where money designated for benefiting society all too often ends up in the hands of extremists.

Taking a number of test cases, he analyzes the Virginia circle of al-Timimi (the so-called Virginia paintball jihadists), and how they came to accept the ideology of Salafism. He also documents a number of different converts to Islam, such as John Walker Lindh, Adam Gadahn and others in an effort to find out how they were inducted into Salafism. In doing all of this, he has gathered together a wealth of information from a wide range of sources for the reader's benefit. His discussion includes even the most recent shooting at Fort Hood, and the American connections of the Yemeni radical Anwar al-Awlaqi whose works inspired the shooter.

Radical Islam in America is an excellent work that discusses a little noticed phenomenon—that Muslim radicals have a wide range of networks, which have been allowed to develop throughout the United States during the past twenty-plus years. More disturbingly, Heffelfinger documents the systematic unwillingness of some Muslim leaders to disassociate themselves from these radicals and to expose them for the dangerous subversives that they are. His work provides a timely warning concerning the future if such networks continue to flourish.

David Cook
Department of Religious Studies
Rice University

A Note on Transliteration

TRANSLITERATIONS FROM the Arabic in this book follow a modified version of the transliteration system of the International Journal of Middle East Studies (IJMES). The IJMES system is the most widely recognized in the field of Middle Eastern and Islamic studies; it is followed here except that no letters are transliterated using diacritical markings, for sake of simplicity. As a result, many names and terms are spelled differently from what one might be accustomed to seeing in the English-language press. For example, I use Usama bin Ladin and al-Qa`ida instead of the more familiar Osama bin Laden and al-Qaeda. In certain cases, Arabic names of individuals and organizations retain their original transliteration spelling rather than being converted to the IJMES standard, when those names were established first in a Western context rather than an Arab one.

Prologue

ON SEPTEMBER 6, 2001, a young man from Marin County, California, arrived in Takhar province in northeastern Afghanistan, volunteering himself as a soldier in the Taliban's war against the Northern Alliance. This man, John Walker Lindh, is now serving a twenty-year term in supermax, the U.S. government's most secure prison, located in Florence, Colorado. Initially charged with ten criminal counts, including conspiring to kill Americans and support terrorists, he accepted a plea agreement, acknowledging guilt of the lesser charges of carrying explosives for and providing aid to the Taliban regime. He is largely kept segregated from the other prisoners, among them some of America's most notorious domestic terrorists: the "Unabomber" Ted Kaczynski and Terry Nichols, convicted in the Oklahoma City bombing of 1995.

But clearly John Walker Lindh was not the hardened criminal mastermind or killer that his fellow prisoners in Supermax were. At the time of his capture by Northern Alliance Forces in late November 2001, Lindh was just twenty years old. He was a sincere believer in the Islamic liberation to which he had committed himself, and felt—like thousands of other aspiring mujahidin—that he was performing his duty to the Islamic community by fighting in Afghanistan. His journey into militant Islam began years earlier, in his quiet town in northern California, and in chat rooms on the Internet.

Born in Washington, DC, on February 9, 1981 to Marilyn Walker and Frank Lindh, John grew up in Takoma Park, and then Silver Spring, two relatively affluent Maryland suburbs of Washington. He attended a program for gifted students at Kensington Parkwood Elementary School, where he was considered highly analytical and observant, even by fourth grade. At age ten, his family relocated to California when his father accepted his law firm's offer to transfer to their San Francisco location.[1] Life in San Anselmo, however, was difficult for John, and he switched in and out of private and public schools in the area. He made few friends and was frequently sick or underweight. Suffering from an intestinal disorder, his parents eventually settled on home schooling, and he ultimately completed his high school equivalency, and Western education, at age sixteen. He asked that the name on his diploma be changed to Suleyman al-Lindh, though he never picked it up.[2]

The portrait of a quiet, intelligent teenager who kept mostly to himself did not then mask a deep, immediate hatred for his country or a desire for violent retribution. He was socially alienated from his peers, but intellectually curious. Although his young man's alienation was arguably self-imposed—at least not imposed by societal confinements—he would eventually learn that he shared this sense of alienation with countless other Muslim youth around the globe. Steadily, John pursued a quest for religious knowledge, and found meaning in Islam—a process undertaken by a great many people, often youth, in the United States and around the world. But what this young man and many others found was a social and political movement masked in religious garb.

John found a source of interest in religion and spiritual matters on the Internet, frequenting chat rooms as he became increasingly drawn to Islam. He posed as rappers on hip-hop websites where he could don assertive and forceful personalities, anonymously. He initially developed an interest in Islam through the biography of Malcolm X and references in hip-hop, common in the stories of many American converts. He was also something of a conspiracy theorist during these years, reading about UFOs, the Illuminati, and the CIA. He read up on other religions as well, but repeatedly his interests returned to Islam. Apparently wary of the sacrifices he may have to endure to convert to Islam, he asked on one discussion board, "Is it okay to watch cartoons?" As he inquired about Islam and the requirements of becoming a Muslim in chat rooms, John sometimes used the screen name Brother Mujahid.[3]

The teenager dressed in a *thawb*, the traditional white, full-length garment worn in the Middle East, and a *kufi*, the prayer cap worn by Muslim men, as he walked around downtown San Anselmo. Thus far self-educated in Islam, John began searching for a place to pray—he first visited the nearby Redwood Mosque, but found it "unorthodox."[4] He subsequently found the Islamic Center of Mill Valley, and performed his *shahada*, or testimony of faith, before two witnesses there, and converted formally, at the age of sixteen. Most striking in this description of his religious quest was this early fundamentalism. Certainly, converts display a zeal for their newfound religion, but typically after conversion, not before.[5] He had established a predetermined set of criteria for his future place of worship, already ascertaining that some Muslims were not on the true path. Was his determination of unorthodoxy at Redwood Mosque based on the Salafi ruling that adornment in the mosque is forbidden? What was his basis for determining what was *halal* (permissible) and *haram* (forbidden) before he had even converted?

Lindh did not fall into Taliban and al-Qa`ida training camps in Afghanistan by happenstance. It was not simply unfortunate timing, but a tide that swept over the world, in the latter half of the twentieth century. And it seems that the teenager from Marin County had been exposed to this form of Islamic activism, Salafism, from his earliest explorations of the faith that he encountered on the Internet.

At the Mill Valley Islamic Center, which primarily served South Asian immigrants, he encountered Tabligh-i-Jamaat, a missionary sect that originated in Pakistan whose name literally means "Proselytizing Group." It is nonviolent and generally apolitical. Tabligh-i-Jamaat, however, is regarded as a peculiar one by most Muslims; in small organized groups, they preach to Muslims on their way to the mosque, roam streets, markets, and go door to door in Muslim neighborhoods pointing out errors in fellow Muslims' practices they deem un-Islamic. The group was founded by a Deobandi cleric in India (a similar sect, but often dubious in the eyes of Salafis); its emphasis is on bringing about the recreation of the Islamic caliphate through Islamic renewal, from the bottom up. Muslims have lost their way and therefore lost their place of power and prestige in the world. Once their practices are corrected and brought back in line with the *Shari`a* (Islamic law), they argue, God will once again support the

Muslims with worldly success. This prescription for curing the ailments of the *umma* (global Muslim community) is strikingly similar to that of the Salafi movement, and many individuals have migrated from one to the next.

Although the Tabligh-i-Jamaat vigorously insists it is nonviolent, the name has been tied to numerous high-profile terrorism cases in the United States and remains an avenue for some Muslims to encounter militant forms of Islam. The Lackawanna Six case, involving Yemeni-American men in upstate New York who sought to join the mujahidin under al-Qa'ida, used the Tabligh-i-Jamaat as their cover for attempting to enter Pakistan and receive paramilitary training in camps there. The list also includes Jose "Omar" Padilla (popularly known as the "dirty bomber"), convicted of conspiracy to commit terrorist acts and currently serving his seventeen-year sentence alongside Lindh in supermax; Richard Reid, who attempted to ignite a shoe bomb on a flight from Paris to Miami in December 2001; Lyman Faris, convicted of planning to bomb the Brooklyn Bridge, and the Portland Seven, accused of attempting to fight U.S. forces in Afghanistan.

John Walker Lindh began spending weekends at the Islamic Center of San Francisco and going on retreats and missionary trips with Tabligh-i-Jamaat, including some outside of the state. On one trip, he made connections to Tabligh-i-Jamaat members who encouraged him to study at a *madrasa*, or Islamic school, in Pakistan. Lindh later followed up on the offer—which ultimately led him to the terrorist training camps in Pakistan and Afghanistan—when he left Yemen in 2000. Three years earlier, his adventure into militant Salafism and jihad began in earnest, though perhaps unknowingly, when he decided to travel to the Middle East to become a serious scholar of Islam.

A year after his conversion, John was intent on advancing his knowledge of Islam through study of the Arabic language. He chose Yemen as his destination, as a place with a rich Islamic history, and far removed from the West in almost every aspect. He arrived there and enrolled at the Yemen Language Center and Center for Arab Studies, the largest of the language schools in Sana'a catering to foreign students, and one the author attended a few months after John departed for Pakistan, in the summer of 2000. The center has two dorms in large, typical Yemeni homes (premodern, seven-story brick buildings) and a third used for classes. The curriculum is much like that found in advanced Arabic programs in the United States, with co-ed classes and accommodations. Lindh complained frequently to the director, Sabri Saleem, and to fellow classmates about various behaviors that he saw as inappropriate in an Islamic country, and harassed them with letters deploring their lack of decency. He was described by Saleem as "a pain in the butt."

In Sana`a, Yemen's capital, he was confused by the peaceful intermingling of Shi`a and Sunni mosques throughout the city, according to his instructors. (The Shi`a of Yemen are Zaydi and make up 25 percent of the total population, largely concentrated in the north of the country, where Sana`a is located.) The Zaydi Shi`a are close theologically to Shafi`i Sunnis, and the two have a history of positive relations of which most Yemenis are proud. Apparently, Lindh found something objectionable about this (Salafi doctrine is persistent in rejecting Shi`a Islam as heretical). While he did explore the traditional mosques in the old city and initially frequented al-Jami` al-kabir (the Grand Mosque) there, he gravitated toward the Salafi teaching to which he was accustomed.

By this time, there were indications of his radicalization, manifest in his changing political views toward the United States and Western aggression. Writing to his mother after the bombings of the U.S. embassies in Nairobi and Dar es Salaam in 1998, he stated that it was more likely that the United States had carried out the attacks itself. Two years later, after the attack on the USS *Cole*, Lindh told his father that by docking the ship in Aden, the United States had declared an act of war that justified the attack. After five weeks of study at the Yemen Language Center, he left the institute, and soon landed on the steps of one of the city's most radical establishments, the Jami`at al-Iman, or Faith University, operated by `Abd al-Majid al-Zindani. Zindani is often described as a loyalist to Usama bin Ladin and was categorized as a Specially Designated Global Terrorist by the U.S. government in 2004. Zindani had also spent significant time in Pakistan and Afghanistan.

The school, comprising approximately 1,000 foreign students, or 25 percent of the student body, was frequently accused of providing an extremist curriculum.[6] It was temporarily closed after 9/11 and numerous foreign students were deported under international pressure for Yemen to crack down on militancy. At the university, Lindh was exposed to jihadi literature, the most moving of which was from Abdullah 'Azzam, the Palestinian jihadi ideologue that also mentored bin Ladin in Afghanistan. During his study at Zindani's university, Lindh also found a mosque on the outskirts of Sana`a practicing the brand of Salafi Islam common to Saudi Arabia, the Ahl al-Khayr mosque. He continued to worship there while studying at Jami`at al-Iman, and appears to have been surrounded by adherents and scholars of Salafi Islam, many with close ties to Saudi Arabia, but also those with previous experience as mujahidin in Afghanistan and other battlefields. Rumors also circulated in Sana`a that Zindani was offering a $500 monthly salary for fighters sent to Bosnia, Chechnya, and other fronts in the jihad.[7]

John returned to California from Yemen for a four-month vacation in 1999, before returning for another planned nine months of study. During his summer vacation, he prayed at a mosque in San Francisco frequented by Salafi Yemenis. During this time, he also met with a band of touring Tabligh-i-Jamaat members he had encountered earlier, one of whom, Khizar Hayat, would later be his first point of contact after he arrived in Islamabad.[8] Just weeks after his return to Yemen, he wrote to Hayat, a businessman and dedicated Tabligh missionary, inquiring about courses of study in Pakistani madrasas. That October, Lindh called Hayat to inform him of his imminent arrival in Islamabad, and asked for a ride to Bannu, five hours away. He was highly selective about his choice of madrasa in Pakistan, and stayed with Hayat for a number of months at his home in Bannu.

Eventually the young "American Taliban," as he would come to be known, enrolled in studies at the Madrasat al-`Arabiyya, in the village of Hasanni Kalan Surani, outside Bannu. He continued his studies there until he began having trouble sleeping in the hot April weather. He wrote to his father, and in the Islamic custom, requested his permission to travel, asking to take leave in the mountains where the weather was cooler. Lindh's next move would take him through Peshawar—the popular staging point for mujahidin traveling from Pakistan's Northwest Frontier Province into Afghanistan in the days of the Soviet jihad—and from there to a training camp where frequent raids into Indian-held Kashmir were made.

The camp that John entered after leaving his madrasa studies in the village outside Bannu was under the Harakat ul-Mujahidin organization, a jihadi group fighting Indian control of Kashmir. It was there, in the early summer of 2001, he learned firsthand of the Taliban movement and made connections with other fighters that would bring him into al-Qa'ida's orbit. After informing these new contacts of his desire to fight alongside the Taliban, he crossed into Afghanistan, reporting to the Dar ul-Anan center for the mujahidin in Kabul.[9] He presented a letter of introduction from his Harakat ul-Mujahidin superiors and said he wanted to fight on the front lines.

Lindh was becoming gradually entrenched in the world of militant jihad, attending al-Qa'ida training camps and staying at guest houses owned by Usama bin Ladin, and in fact met the infamous jihadi leader in person on a few different occasions. Pledging an oath of allegiance (*bay'a*) to bin Ladin and their jihad, John attended the al-Faruq camp to the west of Kandahar, receiving various arms and explosives training. He was asked by one al-Qa'ida officer, Abu Muhammad al-Masri, to conduct operations against the United States or Israel, but Lindh opted to fight in Afghanistan on the front lines.

He traveled around Afghanistan with a group of 150 or so fellow foreign fighters, with an AKM rifle in hand, eventually reaching Takhar in northeastern Afghanistan, where he was ultimately captured by the Northern Alliance when the Taliban fighters he accompanied surrendered in November. They were transported to a prison compound near Mazar-i-Sharif, where Lindh would be interviewed, on November 25, by CIA officer Johnny Spann and another U.S. government employee seeking al-Qa'ida members among the detainees. The following day, Spann was killed as the detainees overpowered their captors and staged an uprising that lasted for several days. Lindh and the other escaped fighters eventually surrendered again to Northern Alliance forces that had cornered them. He returned to the United States wounded, bedraggled, but defiant about the cause to which he had given himself.

In his prepared statement to the court in Alexandria, Virginia, John Walker Lindh told his story, apologetic to the Americans he had so angered, but still believing in the sincerity of the Taliban's jihad as a liberation struggle:

I traveled to Afghanistan in order to assist the Taliban government in opposing the warlords of the Northern Alliance. After being required to take additional military training at a facility in Afghanistan, I volunteered as a foot soldier on the front lines in the province of Takhar, in northeastern Afghanistan. I arrived there on September 6, 2001.

I went to Afghanistan because I believed it was my religious duty to assist my fellow Muslims militarily in their jihad against the Northern Alliance. Because the term "jihad" has been commonly misunderstood, I'd like to take a few minutes to explain the meaning of the term. In the Arabic language, jihad literally means 'struggle.' In Islamic terminology, jihad refers to the spending of one's utmost exertion in the service of God.[10]

John was, like countless others, determined his actions were required as a service to God and community, an obligatory jihad in defense of Islam. This process begins not with the overt recruitment messages found on the Internet and from preachers in the Arab world, but with a much subtler reinterpretation of Islamic teaching—the same John Walker Lindh had been exposed to in his early exploration of Islam in California —taking place in Islamic centers and through Muslim organizations throughout the Western world. That grand Salafi project of reeducation, reshaping the perspectives of Muslims the world over, has been the driver behind the jihadi terrorism with which the United States has been at war for the past decade.

One

WHAT IS SALAFISM?

"Islam began as something strange; and it will return to its original
state of strangeness. Paradise is for the Strangers."

—*The Prophet Muhammad*[1]

THE SALAFI MOVEMENT has been the greatest force for social
change, resistance, and turmoil in the Islamic world over the past two
centuries. Through the collapse of the Ottoman Empire—the last Caliphate to rule over Muslim lands—the bloody end of colonialism, and the
advent of new political identities like Ba'athism and pan-Arabism, a progression of Salafi movements provided an organized response rejecting
modernity and its persistent humiliations. This movement is a call for
traditionalism in its most literal sense—insisting Muslims shun all innovation in religious thought or practice unless it was expressively agreed
upon by the companions of the Prophet (the *sahaba*), those that followed
them (*al-tabi'*) or the generation that succeeded them (*tabi' al-tabi'in*).
These three generations make up what is known as the *Salaf al-salihin*,
or the pious predecessors. And the appeal and persuasive force of Salafi
doctrine lies in the seeming simplicity of its message—the Qur'an and
Sunna, the acts and sayings of the Prophet, along with the consensus
of the pious predecessors, form the sole body of law by which mankind
should be governed.

On the basis of this simple but powerful message aiming to transform the Muslim landscape, Salafi missionaries, educators, preachers, and

1

activists have presented theirs as a movement seeking the humble emula-
tion of these early Muslims who were closest to the Prophet Muhammad,
to reconnect with the original source texts of Islam and cast away any
adulterations. In carrying out this enterprise, however, Salafis have gone
to destructive lengths attempting to purge the global Muslim community
(*umma*) of its impurities. Beyond the physical destruction to tombs and
artifacts they deem idolatrous, contemporary Salafis have laid waste to
the intellectual and cultural establishments of Islamic civilization.

Before moving ahead with a discussion of Salafi mores and their impact on Muslim society, it is necessary to define who exactly Salafis are.
There are a great many Muslim groups today (and even more so over the
past two centuries) that form part of the array of Salafi thinking. The
term "Salafi movement" then refers to this entire range, although most of
those groups cannot be discussed in detail here. Today, many "Wahhabi"
groups label themselves "Salafi," seeing the adjective pejoratively; they
were not followers of ibn 'Abd al-Wahhab's teachings, but of the Salafi
message they taught. For many, but not all, groups, Salafi and Wahhabi
are interchangeable. In the present setting, then, "Salafis" or the "Salafi
movement" are those elements seeking to reform Islamic society, belief,
and practice along their vision of the era of the *Salaf* as an ideal period for
Islam. By its nature, in their view, everything to come after it is progres-
sively worse.

The body of beliefs that make up the Salafi movement were most
comprehensively embodied in the writings of eighteenth-century activist Muhammad ibn 'Abd al-Wahhab. Ibn 'Abd al-Wahhab was born in the
Najd, in eastern modern-day Saudi Arabia, in 1703. His seminal work was
Kitab al-Tawhid (The Book of Monotheism), in which he argued against
what he saw as *bida'* (innovation) and corruption among Muslims, especially from Sufi practices. In attacking the predominant form of Islam of
the day, he also labeled many Muslims *mushrikin* (polytheists) for having
intermediaries to God, believing in saints or holy men, and for a number
of other practices that he considered deviant.[2] Ibn 'Abd al-Wahhab drew
heavily on the prolific writings of thirteenth-century Hanbali scholar Taqi
al-Din ibn Taymiyya. Although Ibn Taymiyya came far after the *Salaf,* Ibn
'Abd al-Wahhab used his writings to support his arguments against the

modern practices of Muslims, especially those on *takfir* (labeling other Muslims disbelievers and thus setting them outside Islam's limits of tolerance).

Within an extremely rigid framework, Ibn `Abd al-Wahhab created an agenda for calling Muslims back to the true Islam. By 1744, he had gained followers in the Najd, but also criticism and challenges from existing Muslim leaders whom he condemned. He sought protection from the powerful tribal family of Al al-Sa`ud, who served as patrons of his teachings and used his following for political support in their revolts against the Ottomans. Throughout the 1800s, these "Wahhabi-Saudi" forces conducted attacks against the Ottomans ruling over the Arabian Peninsula. They were eventually able to hold the provincial capital of Riyadh after a raiding party was led by `Abd al-`Aziz ibn Sa`ud in 1902.

By this time, the teachings of Ibn `Abd al-Wahhab had spread throughout the Peninsula and made their way to other centers of Muslim thought, catapulted by the impact of the Wahhabi-Saudi victory in the Peninsula (and solidified in the coming decades as Ottoman power waned and the Saudis consolidated power over what would become their kingdom).[3] Initially, this Salafi movement, in the early- to mid-eighteenth century, focused almost exclusively on issues of doctrine and worship in the religion, avoiding political rulings or organized social activities. Their primary mission was to call other Muslims back to the true way on the *manhaj al-Salafiyya* (the program of the Salaf); and because of their union with the House of Sa`ud, they remained loyal to their rulers and stayed out of politics.

Salafis reject the existence of multiple sects or denominations of Muslims, arguing that there is only one true way, that of the *Ahl al-Sunna wal-Jama'a* (The People of the Way of the Prophet and the Group [or, Majority]). In accordance with their adherence to the *Salaf,* prominent Salafi scholars have argued that *ijma'* (consensus) is no longer a valid technique in Islamic law, as the gateway of consensus (*abwab al-ijma'*) closed after these three generations, and the work of any subsequent scholars is merely commentary and can not be a binding part of Islamic law or practice. Although the imams of the four schools of thought (Hanafi, Shafi`i, Maliki, and Hanbali) were among the Salaf, the formation of *madhahib* (schools of thought; sing. *madhhab*) occurred after the salaf. Therefore, Salafis adopt no particular *madhhab,* though the vast majority of Sunni Muslims belong to one. In addition, they reject the concept of *ijtihad* (individual interpretation) and *kalam* (mainstream Islamic theology) stating that the Qur'an and *hadith* (sayings of the Prophet), as well as the consensus of the Salaf (this third source is not completely agreed upon among Salafi scholars), are the only legitimate sources for understanding Islamic doctrine.[4]

Further, Salafis reject the doctrine of the Shi'a outright, as well as other sects and movements; especially Sufis, but also modern groups like the Tabligh-i-Jamaat (a popular revivalist movement in South Asia). Salafis have been vehement in their opposition to the many "innovations" in popular religious practice that evolved from Sufism: invocation of Prophets or saints in prayer; visiting graves of saints or Prophets, praying or holding vigils at them; celebrating the *Mawlid* (birthday of Prophet Muhammad); as well as singing, music, photographs, and other practices that had evolved up to that time. In practice, this meant that the followers of Ibn 'Abd al-Wahhab, including the House of Sa'ud, destroyed many Islamic historical sites in the Peninsula on the grounds that they considered them innovations.

There has been widespread demolition of holy sites in lands ruled by the Wahhabi-Saudi forces. Among the most egregious of these, which was undertaken in recent years, was the destruction of the home of Khadija, the first wife of the Prophet. Insult was added to injury with the construction of washrooms and toilets atop the site. The Prophet married Khadija when he was twenty-five and she forty, and she is generally considered to have died in AD 623, at the age of fifty-eight, one year after the *hijra,* the emigration that marked the advent of the Muslim calendar and the establishment of the first Muslim community in Yathrib, which was renamed to al-Madina (Medina, which means "the city," short for *Madinat al-Nabi,* City of the Prophet, or *al-Madina al-Munawwara,* or the Luminous City). Another example of the Salafi demolition project was the removal of part of one of the first mosques built by the Prophet. In early Islamic history, there was a time that Muslims prayed toward Jerusalem before Mecca was established as the *qibla,* or direction of prayer. Masjid al-Qiblatayn, or the Mosque of Two Qiblas, sits in Medina, and is historically significant as it is the only mosque built with two opposing prayer niches within it. The Salafis insisted that the old qibla facing Jerusalem be removed, as it is considered an innovation in religious doctrine to recognize it. Similarly, there was a historical site marking the spot where the Prophet Muhammad alighted from his camel when he first arrived after the Muslims' emigration from Mecca.[5] The site was destroyed as it was considered an innovation to have any construction or adornment on places such as this. This list of demolitions also includes the historical house of Eve, which was located in modern-day Jeddah.[6]

These examples are but a few of the many demolitions "Salafis" have undertaken in recent years, mostly in the Hijaz, the region where Mecca and Medina are located. In sum, the amount to the systematic elimination of any vestiges of diversity or change over time; all things and places must be stripped bare in this effort to rebuild the Muslim umma from its most basic parts—the Qur'an and Sunna alone. (It is no coincidence that "Wahhabi" or Salafi mosques are typically all-white or very sparsely decorated, as they believe adornment in the mosque—and subsequently the entire notion of Islamic sacred art—is considered a sinful innovation.) All this amounts to a culture that is devoid of any markers of its past or progression into the future. It leaves Salafis and the Muslim community they are endeavoring to build anew almost completely dissociated from the modern world.

This dissociation is conceptualized by contemporary Salafis as *ghurba* (estrangement, or life in exile), and in practice entails convincing their supporters they are among the *ghurabaa'* (strangers, but something akin to exiled Puritans) as a means of motivation and reliance on Salafi doctrine to the exclusion of modern thought. Ghurabaa' also refers to the strangeness of true believers in times of corruption (or in the last days, although most Salafis avoid much apocalyptic discourse). It is derived from the hadith: "The Prophet Muhammad said: Islam began as something strange; and it will return as something strange. Paradise is for the Strangers" (reported by Abu Hurayra). His companions then asked: "Who are the Strangers, oh Messenger of God?" He replied: "Those who forbid evil when the people become corrupted." As such, Salafi groups and Salafi mosques often use this term in their names, mission statements, etc., and see themselves as preservers of the true faith while others have abandoned the true practices and worship of Islam.

A clear example of this term in practice is found on the alghurabaa. co.uk website, a group of Muslims in the United Kingdom who have come together to work collectively for the sake of Allah, to dispel all of the lies and fabrications that lead people astray and to expose those who propagate them in order to bring forth the true, orthodox and pure version of Islam as given to us by the Messenger Muhammad and his companions. We adopt the 'aqida of Ahl al-Sunna wa'l-Jama'a referring to the Qur'an and the Sunna of the Messenger Muhammad in accordance with the understanding of the sahaba [companions] and the salaf of this umma only, whilst rejecting all other false and erroneous sources which many have adopted.

Another example, which aptly illustrates Salafi attitudes toward modern practices, is found in an article from the Islamic Thinkers Society, a radical but purportedly nonviolent activist group based in Queens, New York:[7]

The real Ghurabaa' [strangers] do not miss any corruption, culture or tradition (the way many people miss their previous corrupted lifestyles). The Ghurabaa' hate all of that which they used to do and any jahiliyya [ignorance] they come across, hence you never see them voting for man-made law, calling for Freedom, Secularism, Democracy, swearing allegiance to the president and its nation or committing any form of kufr [disbelief] or shirk [polytheism].

To be from this minority we must always keep rejecting anything that is alien to Islam such as the customs of the people: Easter, Valentines Day, Christmas and New-Years, Mothers Day, Fathers Day, Birthdays and any other forms of celebrations or anniversaries that are not from Islam. Al-Nuza' [those who withdraw from society] reject all of this corruption and innovation, and the consequence they will face is severe attack by all people, the so-called "Muslims" (Munafiqin and Fasiqin) [hypocrites and sinners] and non-Muslims.

DEVIATION AND DIVISION

Just as the concept of estrangement has enabled Salafi Muslims to adhere to a strict, demanding ideology throughout trying times, the intensity in that faith—so necessary for such a self-imposed life in exile—has also created divisions within the Salafi movement. The competition over the

claim to inherit Ibn ʿAbd al-Wahhab's message and religious methodology—and to being the true Saved Sect—is fierce, and has led to infighting
and accusations of deviation from the "true" Salafi doctrine. The "Saved
Sect" (or *al-Firqa al-Najiyya*), refers to a saying of the Prophet that is
generally agreed upon by the scholars to say that when Muslims are fragmented into a multitude of falsely guided sects, only one true sect will
enter paradise.[8]

Accordingly, unity in belief is of paramount importance to Salafis, as
Dr. Saleh as-Saleh wrote on the calltoislam.com website:

> The deviation from the *Manhaj* [methodology] of al-Salaf is a very
> serious matter. Muslims know well that the split of this Umma into
> many sects is real and that the protection from this is possible by
> Allah's will once we take by the command of the Prophet: "My way
> and the way of my Sahaba" [the Companions, or first generation of
> Muslims]. It is Sabil al-Mu'minin [The Way of the Believers] whom
> Allah was pleased with and they were pleased with Him.

Despite, or perhaps because of, this intense drive to maintain a single
movement for Salafi reform within Islam, key divisions emerged (from the
early nineteenth century onward) between those Salafis that stayed loyal
to the al-Saʿud and refrained from entering the fray, and those that went
the route of political, social, or militant activism. The original strand of
Saudi Salafis have remained true—at least doctrinally—to rejecting modernity and calling for all Muslims, and all of humanity, to move toward
a world governed by the legal, social, political, and religious framework
(the Shariʿa, or Islamic law, as they interpret it) created during the first
three generations to succeed the Prophet Muhammad. From the beginning, Salafis also thrived from their pact with the House of Saʿud (and subsequent access to oil wealth), which has remained a mutually beneficial
relationship until today. By virtue of being the highest religious authority
presiding over Mecca and Medina, the holiest cities in Islam, they enjoy a
certain de facto legitimacy in Islamic matters.

Since the 1990s, the Salafi clerical establishment in Saudi Arabia has
persistently called for ideological unity, directed primarily at those politically or socially active groups or individuals that were associated with the

term "Salafi." This translated into the use of the Internet for delivering information, beginning in the late 1990s but growing exponentially since then, especially after September 11, 2001. This unified body of clerics—who have effectively overseen the doctrine of the Salafi movement—were ushered in by the creation of the Permanent Committee for Islamic Research and Guidance (*al-lajna al-da'ima lil-buhuth al-'ilmiyya wa'l-ifta'*) by decree of King Faisal in 1971.

The committee was designed to "issue fatwas on individual issues. This is by responding to the fatwa-seeking public in areas of belief, worship, and social issues." The reference to social issues was an indicator of purpose of the committee, which better served the Saudi regime than the Salafi movement, save for the segment of clerics who supported the Royal Family, as they came to be recognized as authorities throughout the Islamic world. 'Abd al-'Aziz ibn Baz (more commonly known as Bin Baz) was perhaps the greatest beneficiary of the new Salafi establishment. He was President of the Islamic University of Medina, one of the two or three elite Salafi Islamic institutions, until 1971. Four years later, he was appointed to the ministerial rank of chair of the Permanent Committee, a position he held until 1993, when he became Grand Mufti of Saudi Arabia until his death in 1999.[9]

One of the criticisms leveled against Bin Baz was the veracity of his *ijaza* (authorization or credentials, which one receives from a teacher as a chain of transmission and proof of their eligibility to teach others). His official obituaries and biographies (*Saudi Gazette, Riyadh Daily*) have stated that he studied under Muhammad ibn 'Abd al-Latif Al al-Shaykh (who is a descendent of Ibn 'Abd al-Wahhab), and Muhammad ibn Ibrahim Al al-Shaykh who was previously Mufti of Saudi Arabia. (Amazingly, both Muhammad ibn Ibrahim Al al-Shaykh and Bin Baz lost their eyesight before the age of twenty). But perhaps more important than his insulated pedigree is that Bin Baz and the Saudi regime effectively institutionalized Salafism by creating a hierarchy of religious offices, officially within the Saudi government. As we will see in later chapters, these institutions played an instrumental role in distributing and embedding the ideology that would form the base of Salafi-jihadi ideology among militants fighting the United States domestically and abroad since the late 1990s.

For the Salafi movement, and for the Saudi government, the death of Bin Baz in May of 1999 was a significant loss (along with the death of his contemporary al-Albani the following October, and also the death of his student and member of the Permanent Committee Muhammad al-Uthaymin—both of whom were major figures in Salafi jurisprudence). The diminished legitimacy of the Saudi Salafi establishment has made for a tenuous situation, as those on the *manhaj al-Salaf* may question the Saudi regime's motives and involvement with the Permanent Committee and other religious offices, and in turn question what the true stance on political or militant resistance for a Muslim today should be. While Bin Baz engaged in bitter exchanges on issues of beliefs and worship, he was also criticized in the Muslim world for supporting the Saudi government throughout the Gulf War, including when they imprisoned fellow Salafis for opposing the regime's position. The generation of Salafi students to succeed Bin Baz have followed the same pattern; condemning al-Qa'ida in the Peninsula while supporting the right for Muslim resistance in Iraq.

Usama bin Ladin came to see Bin Baz as purely a puppet of the Saudi regime, as he described him—and the Saudi involvement among the Salafi scholars in the kingdom—in a 1996 interview with the now defunct Australian-based *Nida' al-Islam* (call of Islam, http://www.islam.org.au):

> "[T]he regime has strived to keep these [honest] scholars in the shadows and then removed them, one way or another, from being effective elements in the lives of the people in the community. At the forefront of these scholars was the Sheikh Abdullah Bin Hamid—May Allah bless his soul—who was the Mufti in the Arabian Peninsula, and who headed the supreme council of judges. However, the regime constrained him and tightened their grip on him until he offered his resignation. He has many famous writings in response to the unacceptable laws which the government had introduced instead of the Law of Allah, one of these is a treatise dealing with the law of work and workers which deals with many of the introduced laws which contradict the law of Allah.
>
> At the same time, they promoted some of the scholars who were far below Sheikh Ibn Hamid—may Allah bless his soul—those who have been known to be weak and soft, so they put them forward in a cunning plan which began more than twenty years ago. During the preceding two decades, the regime enlarged the role of Bin Baz

(Grand Mufti) because of what it knows of his weakness and flexibility and the ease of influencing him with the various means which the interior ministry practices through providing him with false information. So, a generation of youth was raised believing that the most pious and knowledgeable of people is Bin Baz as a result of the media promotion through a well-studied policy, which had been progressed over twenty years.

After this, the government began to strike with the cane of Bin Baz, every corrective programme which the honest scholars put forward, further, it extracted a Fatwa to hand over Palestine to the Jews, and before this, to permit entry into the country of the two sacred mosques to the modern day crusaders under the rule of necessity, then it relied on a letter from him to the minister for internal affairs and placed the honest scholars in the gaols. (Translation by the Australian staff of *Nida' al-Islam*)

Not surprisingly, in bin Ladin's biography, *Nida' al-Islam* described his outlook as "[t]he way of the people of Sunna and Jama'a in accordance with the understanding of the righteous predecessors, in total and in detail. From this emerges the necessity for armed struggle preceded by Da'wa and military preparation in order to repel the greater Kufr, and to cooperate with Muslims in order to unite their word under the banner of monotheism, and to set aside divisions and differences."

Usama bin Ladin's struggle with the Saudi Salafi establishment was a prototypical example of the internal struggle for the one true interpretation of the "pious predecessors" (the salaf) and the claim to represent the people of "al-Sunna wal-Jama'a," which roughly translates as representing the majority view. Both Bin Baz and bin Ladin argued unwaveringly for a single, unified movement for Muslims to confront the challenges of modernity. This recent argument played itself out in the previous century, however, as Muslim movements, including the *Salafiyya,* were forced to decide upon acceptable, "Islamic" solutions to political, social, and cultural crises that challenged their identity as Muslims.

In the late 1850s, the bright young Persian-born Muhammad ibn Safdar Husayni, better known as Jamal al-Din al-Afghani, was serving as a counselor to the Awadh King in Delhi, India. After coming into conflict with the ruler, he was sent to Afghanistan, where he was unable to gain a steady foothold into local politics. Al-Afghani's next destination was Istanbul, where he embraced as patron the politician-reformer Ali Pasha. But more importantly, while in Istanbul, he met Muhammad 'Abduh, and through him circles of students at the renowned al-Azhar University in Cairo.[10]

Al-Afghani, who likely began his Islamic education as a Shi'a, or at least he appears to have gained much of his education from Shi'a institutions, was far more politically driven than doctrinally obsessed. In fact, al-Afghani's methodology included theology, philosophy, jurisprudence, and mysticism.[11] The Wahhabis' Salafi-inspired reform movement that began in the Arabian Peninsula a century earlier rejected the use of philosophy and reasoning as unnecessary innovations, and the practice of mystics (Sufism) to be as deviant as idolatry. Jurisprudence was relegated to the Qur'an, Sunna of the Prophet, and the consensus opinion of the Salaf; any approach beyond those sources was rejected. Nevertheless, while today's best known Salafis are heirs to the movement of Ibn 'Abd al-Wahhab, the broader Muslim world, as well as the West, became familiar with "Salafi" as an Islamic reform movement through the speeches and publications of al-Afghani and 'Abduh.

The unity of the Salafi movement, if it can even be seen as a whole, has faced considerable challenges as influential reformers attempt to implement their idea of change. Muslims across the Middle East and South Asia felt the currents of Salafism and the spirit of revivalism that accompanied it. Yet, without an official body or political entity to embody the movement, Salafis had no way to ensure conformity or uniformity among subsequent scholars and reformers who heard their call. The term 'Salafi' is indeed most frequently associated in the nineteenth century with the movement started by Jamal al-Din al-Afghani and his disciple Muhammad 'Abduh. Their Salafi movement, however, was considered liberal by many Western observers and historians of the time, as it incorporated modern methodologies to achieving change in a broader quest to rid the Muslim world of colonialism (e.g., printing periodicals, state diplomacy, advocating activism, and mass mobilization). During this era, al-Afghani and 'Abduh's Salafism dominated the politically inactive religiosity of the Salafis in the Arabian Peninsula (that would change of course after the discovery of oil beneath Saudi Arabia in 1930s). This global Islamic call rejuvenated the ailing Muslim community, and spawned two of the most influential organized political movements of the following century: Abul'-A'la Mawdudi (1903–1979), founder of Pakistan's Jamaat-e-Islami and Hasan al-Banna (1906–1949), founder of the Muslim Brotherhood in Egypt. Mawdudi was born in India and formed Jamaat-e-Islami, working tirelessly to create an Islamic state after Pakistan's independence in 1947. Al-Banna established the Muslim Brotherhood and created a discourse on Islam and modernity that has affected virtually all of the modern-day mujahidin movements. Accordingly, this trend of Salafism overshadowed the tumultuous landscape of the nineteenth- and twentieth-century Islamic world.

Two

SALAFISM AND THE REDEFINITION OF MUSLIM IDENTITY

"So long as humanity exists, the struggle will not cease between dog-
ma and free investigation, between religion and philosophy; a desper-
ate struggle in which, I fear, the triumph will not be for free thought,
because the masses dislike reason."[1]

—*Jamal al-Din al-Afghani*

IN A TONE ALMOST UTTERLY opposing that of the "Wahhabis," al-
Afghani argued in favor of Islam's civilizational significance, as the absorber
of foreign sciences and philosophy, Greek and Persian assimilation, and
ultimately, as a means to engage in the modern world as Muslims, rather
than retreat from it. Clearly, contemporary Salafi movements are staunchly
opposed to any foreign contamination like that al-Afghani boasted of, and
have fought doggedly to purge these "innovations" from Islamic practice and Muslim culture. Throughout the late 1880s, the Saudi-Wahhabi
forces were bogged down in political and military campaigns against the
Rashidi dynasty in the Najd; by 1884, however, Jamal al-Din al-Afghani
and Muhammad `Abduh arrived in Paris and began publishing their peri-
odical that would influence a generation of reformers.[2]

While all Salafi movements have called for unity among the ranks of
Muslims, most have done so while maintaining the exclusivity of theirs
as the only correct doctrine. Al-Afghani, however, appealed for Muslim
unity by arguing the Muslims' shared values and shared danger from outside threats should outweigh differences over doctrine; in essence, he

accepted the diversity of thought and downplayed differences toward the
end goal of unity and collaborative activism. Although al-Afghani was not
truly liberal in his views (he was not a proponent of constitutional democracy or parliament, he mainly sought to unseat unjust rulers and expel
foreign enemy elements from Arab and Muslim lands), he was certainly a
progressive voice for Islamic revivalism. So much so, in fact, that he was
viewed with concern by later Muslim reformers as a voice in favor of science over religion.

Speaking of the period in Paris, after al-Afghani and 'Abduh began
publishing *al-'Urwa al-Wuthqa* (The Indissoluble Bond), the scholar Albert Hourani wrote,

> At this point we become aware of a novelty in al-Afghani's thought,
> or at least a new emphasis. The centre of attention is no longer Islam
> as a religion, it is rather Islam as a civilization. The aim of man's act
> is not the service of God alone; it is the creation of human civiliza-
> tion flourishing in all its parts.[3]

In reference to al-Afghani's change in beliefs after his arrival in Paris,
the influential Salafi reformer Rashid Rida wrote in 1923, "[He] became
a rebel against religion, and came to believe it was the enemy of science,
reason, and civilization so much so that he gladly and deferentially ac-
quiesced in Renan's attack on Islam."[4] Al-Afghani came to believe that
philosophy, which should be based on the findings of modern science and
technology, should drive Islamic thought. His "modern Islamic philosophy" was a force for synthesizing Islamic identity with the modern age,
but also earned him many critics.[5] While al-Afghani had an unmistak-
able impact on Islamic revival and reform at the end of the nineteenth
century, his advocating science, technology, reason, and arts (or what we
would today consider social sciences) of non-Islamic origins was not to
last. His heirs took up his early message of Islamic resistance to Western
imperialism, and looked more earnestly back to the model of the *Salaf* for
solutions to their contemporary dilemmas.

Muhammad 'Abduh (1849–1905) referred to his movement as Salafi,
with an agenda for confronting Western imperialism and reforming Islamic society at once. 'Abduh argued that the early generations of Muslims

(*al-salaf al-salihin*) had produced a vibrant civilization because they had creatively interpreted the Qur'an and hadith to answer the needs of their time. This reinterpretation of Salafi doctrine was a powerful unifying force between pan-Islamic nationalists less concerned with doctrinal conformity, as well as those following a Salafi model of Islam. This Islamist trend, largely under 'Abduh (and the enduring influence of al-Afghani, even after his death in 1897) took an almost accepting view of modernity, seeking to demonstrate Islam's compatibility with European rationalism. 'Abduh's Salafi movement allowed for *ijtihad,* or independent interpretation of sacred texts, to arrive at a legal decision.[6] The dominant Salafi ideologues today generally accept only the Qur'an, hadith, and the consensus of the *salaf* as valid sources of law, thus enshrining a rigid conservatism and literal interpretation of the texts.

'Abduh came from a well-regarded family in the Nile River delta, near Tanta. As a youth, he was resistant toward, and ultimately tried to escape from, the rote memorization and rigid doctrines of the *madrasa* (Islamic school) in Tanta where he studied. But 'Abduh credits an uncle of his for revealing to him the true belief in God and the freedom of a life of knowledge and contemplation. Like al-Afghani, he was favorable to mysticism and the philosophy of Sufis (in fact this was a shared passion for the two that partially sparked their relationship).[7] When al-Afghani settled in Egypt in 1871, 'Abduh quickly became his most dedicated student, and 'Abduh delved into texts on civilizations and philosophy. He was deeply moved by Francois Guizot's *History of Civilizations in Europe* and famous Arab philosopher and historian Ibn Khaldoun's *Muqaddima,* both of which dealt with the rise and fall of civilizations.

Al-Afghani and 'Abduh were at the forefront of Egyptian politics, and by extension those of the British and French Empires in the Middle East. 'Abduh expressed his and his teacher's ethos in a series of articles in the newly formed *al-Ahram* publication. Following the British invasion and occupation of Egypt in 1882, 'Abduh was arrested, jailed for a time, and exiled from Egypt. After a short sojourn in Beirut, he arrived, along with the exiled al-Afghani, in Paris in 1884. After four years in Paris, 'Abduh returned to Cairo where he served as a judge for several years before becoming the highest ranking figure at one of Sunni Islam's most prestigious institutions—the al-Azhar University. Unlike future Salafi figures such as

Sayyid Qutb, 'Abduh and his movement sought gradual reform, and as Grand Mufti of Egypt, 'Abduh's Salafi movement focused on education and da'wa (proselytizing).[8]

After his time in Paris, during which he made a failed attempt to enter Tunis in disguise in an attempt to access Sudan—one of al-Afghani's poorly thought out political schemes (the two had also begun a secret Muslim society in Paris)—'Abduh returned, Beirut where he lectured for three years.[9] These lectures formed the basis of his most significant literary work, *Risalat al-Tawhid* (Letter of Unity), which dealt largely with the issue of inner decay of the Muslim body, a topic al-Afghani also repeatedly drew on. In 1888, he was allowed to return to Egypt and became a judge soon after. In 1899, he became Mufti of Egypt (the highest Islamic legal position). In this capacity, he attempted to reform the national law along salafi precepts and doctrine; in essence, to Islamize the state from the inside. Hourani succinctly concludes, "'Abduh's purpose, in all the acts of his later life as well as his writings, was to bridge the gulf within Islamic society, and in so doing, to strengthen its moral roots."[10] Along these lines, 'Abduh sought to determine what exactly Islam meant in the modern world, a task which he strived toward, nonviolently until his death in 1905.

Like Wahhabi, clerics and their followers in nineteenth-century Arabia, Salafi reformers of the al-Afghani-'Abduh mold sought to legitimize themselves by affiliation with and textual support from thirteenth-century scholar Ibn Taymiyya.[11] In the late 1800s, as such, there was a vibrant renewal project—in Baghdad, Damascus, India, and Arabia—to locate rare original manuscripts of Ibn Taymiyya's writings and copy and provide commentary on the known and cataloged texts. Thus, by the end of al-Afghani's life, the center of gravity for Salafi reform had again returned to essential, detailed doctrinal questions on the Salaf (akin to the American debates over the intent of the framers of the Constitution)—the clamoring for ideological legitimacy under Ibn Taymiyya's shadow is illustrative of this endeavor.

Meanwhile, in Arabia, a rival to the Sa'ud family, that of Ibn Rashid, was ruling most of the Najd throughout the 1880s. In 1884, as al-Afghani and 'Abduh began their enterprise in Paris, the Saudi-Wahhabi forces were soundly defeated by the Rashidis. The ruling Muhammad ibn

Rashid, however, did not attempt to stamp out the Wahhabi-Salafi reform movement, but rather, quite disastrously, ignored it.[12] The ideological underpinnings of the Saudi family's strength and base of support lay with the Salafi doctrine, and their austere vision of society reconstructed through a seventh-century lens. The death of Ibn Rashid in 1897 gave the exiled 'Abd al-Rahman Al al-Sa'ud (then living in Kuwait) means to reenter the Najd and attempt to reclaim rule over the dynasty his grandfather started. After a series of bloody battles, the warring sides (which by then had come to include the waning Ottoman Empire), came to an agreement wherein al-Sa'ud was named deputy governor of the Najd, but still under Turkish rule.[13]

In 1913 after years of negotiations, the Ottomans and British signed the Anglo-Turkish Convention, dividing the Arabian Peninsula from the Qatar Peninsula to Yemen, which included Riyadh, the base of Wahhabi-Saudi power, declaring it under Turkish rule. The following year, Ibn Sa'ud signed a pact formalizing his status as a subject and instrument of the Turkish state, but meanwhile, the head of the Sa'ud family looked elsewhere for support, to India, and also Britain, with whom he signed a treaty in December 1915, recognizing him as independent ruler of the Najd.[14] In the following years, the British sent hefty subsidies of currency, arms, and men to Ibn Sa'ud, even as they were subsidizing his rival, Sharif Hussayn, ruler of Mecca, to lead an Arab revolt against Turkish rule of the Two Holy Shrines, Mecca and Medina.[15] Until the early 1920s Saudi-Wahhabi forces made gains in the Peninsula, including the area of the Hijaz, surrounding Mecca. In 1922, Ibn Sa'ud's forces took the logistically valuable port of Abha, on the southeastern coast along the Red Sea.[16] Two short years later, Ibn Sa'ud would take Mecca as World War I took place a continent away.

The Salafi current of Muhammad 'Abduh was continued by his leading student, Rashid Rida (1865–1935), who published a pan-Islamist message through the magazine *al-Manar* until his death.[17] He blamed the Muslim world's weakness vis-à-vis the West on excesses of the Middle Ages, influences of European philosophers, and other "deviations" which led the Muslim nation to fall out of God's favor. His work sought to purify Muslims in order to bring about an Islamic revival that would lead ultimately to political success. This concept of the exemplary purity of the early Islam of the Salaf is a doctrinal pillar for a range of Salafi groups that emerged

after this era, from the Saudi Salafi establishment heir apparent to Ibn
'Abd al-Wahhab, to political Islamists at odds with their governments,
to militant Salafi ideologues. With 'Abduh and Rida, the model for Is-
lamic revival and reform was established and became widely regarded as
"Salafi," and its implementation by the succeeding generation of Egyptian
Islamist activists brought it into direct conflict with the state.

Rida was born in Ottoman Syria, in the city of Tripoli, and studied
under the Turkish system where he learned French.[18] Rida took his interest in Sufism (having long been enchanted by Imam Ghazali, one of the
preeminent figures in medieval Sufism) and entered into the Naqshbandi
Sufi brotherhood, where he heartily adopted the ascetic practices pre-
scribed to its followers. After an encounter with whirling dervishes, whom
he found to be making a joke of their religion, his sympathies swung toward the Salafi-Wahhabi current, and the scholarship of Ibn Taymiyya
(who had also belonged to a Sufi brotherhood at one time).[19] But Rida's
real passion in Islam was ignited when he first read 'Abduh and al-Afghani's journal,

> I found several copies of the journal among my father's papers, and
> every number was like an electric current striking me, giving my
> soul a shock, or setting it ablaze, and carrying me from one state to
> another . . . no other Arabic discourse in this age or the centuries
> which preceded it has done what it did in the way of touching the
> seat of emotion in the heart and persuasion in the mind.[20]

Profoundly moved by the works of 'Abduh and al-Afghani, Rida had
also become a proponent of the Salafi-Wahhabi doctrine (as was made
clear in his work, *al-Wahhabiyyun wa'l-Hijaz* (the Wahhabis and the Hijaz), in which he supported the Wahhabi-Saudi quest to rule Mecca. Ibn
Sa'ud gained a great popular advantage, too, in winning over the publisher
of *al-Manar,* with its wide, pan-Islamic readership. The working relationship between Rida and Ibn Sa'ud translated into a source of funding for
the former, through which the former publicized the Salafi cause, replete
with a Muslim Congress held in Mecca in 1926 (which amounted to nothing—the forerunner of many similar, subsequent conventions sponsored
by the House of Sa'ud). It was the first attempt of by Ibn Sa'ud to court

the Muslim public, through its scholars, to accept their Salafi doctrine as mainstream.[21]

Here, one sees the predominant strains of Salafi reform, that begun by Ibn ʿAbd al-Wahhab in extreme rigidity, and that advanced by al-Afghani, espousing science and philosophy, reconverge with Rashid Rida. These currents, separated by a wide gulf (given the distance between Wahhabi clerics and al-Afghani and even ʿAbduh in the nineteenth century), re-united amid the concurrent Saudi-Wahhabi conquest of Arabia and rule over Mecca. But most important, it ushers in a return to the earlier con-ceptualization of Salafism that arose in eastern Arabia under Ibn ʿAbd al-Wahhab in the late eighteenth century, of doctrinal scrutiny and intra-Islamic purification. This convergence marked a critical moment for the Salafi movement as a whole, as it was now oriented toward tackling con-temporary political issues while maintaining its doctrinal exactitude and rejection of foreign, corrupting innovations.

For al-Afghani, ʿAbduh, and Rida, Islamic Mysticism, or Sufism, had begun them on a deeper and more introspective path to Islam and episte-mology. But all three diverged from that path and favored activist reform based on the models of the salaf. As some of the most influential Muslim thinkers of these centuries, their lives demonstrate much of the internal Islamic struggle for identity amid modernity that Muslims the world over experienced. That internal conflict—over, fundamentally, what Islam is and how best to act in the world—remains at the heart of the Salafi move-ment, and perhaps for that reason, enjoys continued attention and inter-est from the Muslim world and its observers.

Hasan al-Banna (1906–1949), like Muhammad ʿAbduh, moved to Cairo at a relatively young age to pursue higher Islamic education. Be-tween 1923 and 1928, when he founded the *Ikhwan al-Muslimun* (the Muslim Brotherhood), al-Banna immersed himself in Rida's teachings and the currents of the Salafi movement near Dar al-ʿUlum university, where he studied.[22] Al-Banna sought to confront Western influence by mobiliz-ing Muslims toward a (re)awakening of Islamic values and a rejection of secularism. Al-Banna followed in Rida's footsteps in this respect, seeing a societal drift away from Islam as the source of law and societal norms, with the West, or more accurately European colonialist powers, playing a central role in this process of Islamic decline.

Early in the Muslim Brotherhood's history, political and social mobilization was of primary concern to al-Banna. The Society of Muslim
Brothers was only one of a number of organizations al-Banna organized in
the late 1920s, but by 1932 he focused his efforts on the Brotherhood. In
1932, al-Banna, who had founded the organization from the Suez Canal
city of Isma'iliyya, decided to relocate to Cairo, where he incorporated
an Islamic society led by one of his brothers.[23] It soon began publishing
its first weekly newsletter and by 1938 had grown to have three hundred
branches and and between 50,000 and 150,000 members.[24]

From the 1930s to the 1950s, the organization continued to grow rapidly, initially as an apolitical movement dedicated to religious revival and
reform. By the 1940s the organization gravitated toward political dissent,
leveling criticism at the British administration in control of the country
in newsletters and at rallies.[25] In 1941 the Brotherhood fielded candidates
for parliamentary elections on a platform centered largely on a demand
that the British military withdraw from Egypt. Their initiatives prompted
an order for al-Banna's exile from Egypt by British authorities that same
year, and he was imprisoned months later, along with other Brotherhood
leaders. Distracted by World War II, the British administration lifted some
of the earlier measures, and the organization grew to be the largest organized force in Egypt by 1949, when it counted between 300,000 and
600,000 members.[26]

The society grew despite being officially banned and dissolved in
1948, followed by another wave of imprisonments against the Brothers.
These crackdowns prompted a violent reaction from the organization,
whose members were responsible for the assassination of Egyptian Prime
Minister Mahmud Fahmi al-Nuqrashi Pasha, who had ordered the dissolution. Al-Banna was himself assassinated two months later.[27] These
assassinations foreshadowed greater acts of political violence to come for
the Brotherhood and Egyptian Islamists. Two years after the Free Officers coup of 1952 led by Gamal Abdel Nasser, six leaders of the Muslim
Brotherhood were hung, while thousands of others served difficult prison
sentences.[28] Following the tremendous blow of al-Banna's death to the
organization, the Muslim Brothers reorganized and prepared for greater
confrontation with the political authority in Egypt.

SALAFI EVOLUTION IN EGYPT

The model of Salafi reform in Egypt in the early nineteenth century did a great deal to influence Muslim identity in coming decades. As the Brotherhood was dispatching fighters to Palestine in the late 1940s, its ideologues—and Salafi thinkers more broadly—were developing a doctrine for Islamist activism that went beyond Egypt. This doctrine was carried into Europe in the 1950s where many of the Ikhwan sought refuge after purges in their native Egypt, particularly in Germany and the United Kingdom. The ideology was also transported to America, where it had an enduring impact on Islamic activism and community organizing. By and large, the mainstream Ikhwani doctrines that developed in the West in the 1950s–60s was nonviolent, characterized by education and youth programs and a drive to preserve Islamic culture (as seen through their lens) among Muslim immigrant communities. And while the Brotherhood can be considered one branch of Salafism, others developed along their own trajectories in Egypt, several with more violent calls for action in their quest to establish Islamic law as the rule in their society.

Egypt served as the wellspring for modern Islamism and has witnessed more than a century of evolving Salafi thought and activism. It has produced some of the most influential Islamist thinkers and organizers of recent history—Muhammad ʾAbduh, Rashid Rida, Hasan al-Banna, and Sayyid Qutb—who collectively dealt with issues of Islamic reform and revivalism, modeled on Salafi ideals. In recent decades, it has also produced or trained leading jihadi figures such as Ayman al-Zawahiri, ʾAbdullah ʾAzzam, and ʾUmar ʾAbd al-Rahman. These figures have a tremendous influence on the formation of contemporary Muslim identity; all had the common goal of confronting modern society, and attempting to find the proper place for Islam within it. Egyptian thinkers and activists have maintained a leading role in the currents of Islamism, they themselves being the founders of Islamist activism in the late nineteenth and twentieth centuries.

Muhammad ʾAbd al-Salam al-Faraj, an engineer by trade who was vital to the Egyptian Salafi movement of the 1960s and executed in 1982, was inspired by the Salafi models of change put forth by Sayyid Qutb, and Rida before him. As is evident by the period after Sayyid Qutb, a majority of Salafis internationally proclaimed to be of the opinion that revolution and/or violent resistance are necessary measures for bringing about change. Faraj clashed with another rising militant Islamist group, Takfir wa'l-Hijra (Excommunication and Emigration) led by Shukri Mustafa; Faraj viewed them as literally fleeing in the face of confrontation with the enemy (hearkening back to an earlier dynamic between al-Afghani and the Wahhabi visions of engagement with the modern world). For Faraj—as he laid out in his best-known work, al-Farida al-Ghayba, or "The Neglected Duty"—armed jihad had been neglected by Muslims, and must be renewed and understood as an obligation for every believer, like fasting, prayer, and alms giving (zakat).[29] This form of militant Salafism was a prominent successor to the widely popular Salafi reform movement embodied by Rashid Rida and Hasan al-Banna.

Egypt passed through a turbulent and violent period that saw militant Islamists targeting the ruling government. The 1981 assassination of President Anwar Sadat by the al-Jihad organization, and a spree of jihadi violence in the 1990s, culminating in the 1997 attack against tourists at Luxor, were among the most vigorous episodes of internal unrest in the country. Armed Islamists sought to create a new legal and social structure in Egypt through violent tactics, but public opinion decidedly turned against them, effectively halting their campaign. The gruesome attack on tourists at Luxor damaged the Egyptian reputation, and likewise, the national economy, which was largely dependent on tourism dollars. Today, the Salafi model for social change and Islamic renewal continues in a variety of forms in Egypt, and in the majority of cases it is advanced by groups with nonconfrontational agendas. Current strains in Egyptian Salafi thinking appear to be dominated by doctrinal issues and scholarly debate rather than political or social action. An example of this is found on the Salaf Misr website [misr is Arabic for Egypt], which hosts several discussions of more militant Salafis, such as the campaign in Somalia against Ethiopia, but avoids discussion on such power struggles within Egypt. The sense is that for most contemporary Salafi groups, instilling a literal and strict adherence to issues of faith and doctrine—and expounding on them at length—takes precedence over organized or militant Islamist activity. Preachers such as Hasan bin `Abd al-Wahhab Marzuq al-Banna, Abu Muhammad Khalid bin `Abd al-Rahman, Khalid `Uthman, and others with local followings are distributed on Islamist web forums, where users discuss particular aspects of the Salafi doctrine and how it should be defined. This practice, known as *jarh wa'l-ta'dil* (Refutation and Revision, e.g., internal Salafi challenges over various doctrinal issues), is a seemingly endless process, which often seems to drive Salafi activists further apart rather than create unity or consensus. For example, an essay from Egyptian Salafi shaykh Muhammad Sa'id Raslan, reads, "Is this from the Salafiyya?! Our doctrine regarding Divine Judgment and Destiny," and provides a lengthy discussion on the "proper" Salafi view toward such matters.[30] Doctrinal infighting has indeed become a defining trait among the competing branches of Salafism.

Moving back from today's Salafi landscape, however, one observes that individuals and groups driven toward more immediate social and political change were less compelled to engage in doctrinal infighting, and focused their efforts on militant campaigns against the perceived enemies of Islam. Abdullah 'Azzam, who completed his PhD in Islamic jurisprudence at al-Azhar University in Cairo in 1973, earned his scholarly credentials in the Egyptian intellectual climate before leaving to teach and organize Muslim Brothers in Amman, Jordan, in the later 1970s.[31] Al-Qa'ida's deputy leader, Ayman al-Zawahiri, was arrested following the crackdown on Islamists after Sadat's assassination, although he was never charged in connection with the assassination plot.[32] Another Egyptian militant leader, Rifa'i Ahmad Taha, was an early supporter of Usama bin Laden, and a signatory to his 1998 fatwa establishing the "International Front Against Crusaders and Jews," the formal beginnings of al-Qa'ida.

From the doctrine-focused ideologues active in chat rooms, to the evolving mass movement of the Muslim Brotherhood, to militant activists engaged in combat against tyrannical governments at home and abroad, Salafism evolved into a diverse array of activist groups in Egypt. From where it developed and emerged, these Salafi groups were more influential than any other Islamic organizations in formulating Muslim identity in the twentieth century. Most notably, they bridged Islamist activism with what it means to be Muslim. Generations of reformers succeeded in instilling the notions of Salafism as a purification and remedy for the modern ailments of the Islamic society. This transformation paved the way for jihadi violence, whose practitioners built their legitimacy around ideological adherence to Salafi Islam.

Three

IDEAS TRANSFORMED INTO ACTION

"If we insist on calling Islamic Jihad a defensive movement, then we must . . . mean by it 'the defense of man' against all those elements which limit his freedom."

—*Sayyid Qutb*

THE PRECEDING TWO CHAPTERS have attempted to trace the path of Salafism, a reform movement constructed of sometimes-conflicting concepts of the generation of the *Salaf,* and certainly conflicting agendas on how to achieve the desired change—to bring back the true Islam—in contemporary society. The focus has been on influential figures, mostly Muslim intellectuals, who shaped the landscape, giving of course inadequate attention to the role of religious societies and the individual Muslim. But at this juncture—following the assassination of al-Banna in 1949 and the dissolution of the Brothers as an organization in Egypt a year earlier—a looming crisis was created for the movement. It now had no legitimate routes to resistance available to it in its primary arena—Egypt. It is here where small groups and underground organizations of Muslims come to play an increasingly critical, and violent, role in Salafi activism.

Stepping back, we see that the preceding two centuries of the Salafi movement were characterized by contentious debate, directed at both other, self-proclaimed Salafis as well as fellow Muslims adhering to other doctrines. The era of the 1960s, epitomized by Sayyid Qutb and to a lesser extent, Abu'l-A'la Mawdudi, were characterized by action. Qutb, after his formative education period, dedicated himself to societal and political change, insisting that Muslims had lived in ignorance and now needed to reclaim their right to live under an Islamic government under Shari'a law (also believing that Islam was a comprehensive way of life that should be adopted by all mankind). Qutb, unlike his immediate Salafi predecessors al-Afghani, 'Abduh, Rida, and al-Banna, was radical in his language, calling for Muslims to govern themselves under Islamic law, going so far as to say Islam ceases to exist on earth when Muslims do not implement its code in their society and daily lives. But Sayyid Qutb was a complicated and troubled figure who seemed bent on martyrdom as his best contribution to the long-term success of the Islamic resistance, and he was right.

A famous tale of Ibn Taymiyya's end states that he wrote day and night in his prison cell until his jailors finally took his pen away, and he died days after, a man simply incapable of life without the written word. Sayyid Qutb seemed to follow in this mold to a tee, although his death sentence was announced to him in 1965, to which he famously responded, "Thank God, I performed jihad for fifteen years until I earned this martyrdom."[1] Qutb was a prolific and undying voice for the Salafi movement he inherited—mainly from Hasan al-Banna, in his view at least—and was determined to rouse Muslims from their state of ignorance. The term *jahliyya* is used throughout Qutb's writing. Indeed it is a critical theme, referring to the era before Islam, which is known as jahliyya, or ignorance. Its use implies that Qutb perceived Muslims as having lapsed into a state of disbelief, or nominal belief, wherein they did not actually live under Islamic law or even Islam's code of conduct. It would prove to be a radical shift in language from one who would become the leading voice for Islamic resistance in the world.

Sayyid Qutb was born in the northern Egyptian village of Musha, on October 9, 1906. After completing college, he worked in the Ministry of Education in Cairo beginning in 1939.[2] He has come to be known best for his lasting influence on Usama bin Ladin and Ayman al-Zawahiri. But his journey from intellectual to a proponent of militancy began in 1948 when he arrived in the United States, first for graduate studies at Colorado State, then later working in Washington, DC. Upon his return to Egypt in 1950, he promptly resigned from government service (which had amply subsidized him as a student in the United States)[3] and joined the Muslim Brotherhood. He had learned of al-Banna's death while in America. The two had never met, but knew each other through reputation, and, following Qutb's hanging in 1966, his brother Muhammad went to great lengths, as a scholar in his own right, to defend Sayyid's dedication to al-Banna's vision of the Muslim Brothers.

In 1949 Sayyid Qutb published his first book, *Social Justice in Islam*, while he was living in Colorado. Like many of his fellow Islamists, Qutb expected the Free Officers to create, or make steps toward, Islamic rule in the country. Gamal Abdel Nasser, the eventual antihero to the Salafiyya in Egypt, refused to institute Shari`a law, and his brief alliance with the Brotherhood came to an abrupt end. Qutb was among those caught up in the crackdown in 1954; and he was imprisoned for ten years as an enemy of the regime. Freed in 1964, he was rearrested within a matter of months, and tried, this time with much public attention, for sedition. He was hanged on August 29, 1966 for his alleged involvement in an assassination attempt on President Abdel Nasser. During his time in prison, however, he wrote his most influential works, continuing his calls for an Islamic state rooted in a revival of true Islamic practices and beliefs.

The saga of Sayyid Qutb and his defiance of the Egyptian regime created a hero for Islamist activists, and his *Milestones (Ma'alim fi'l-tariq)*, continues to be a primer for Muslims seeking to alter society and reorient it on an Islamist trajectory. In that book, he lays out the characteristics of the Islamic nation, and describes everything outside of it as jahiliyya, "[f]or human life, there is only one true system, and that is Islam; all other systems are Jahiliyyah."[4] Qutb's call for a vanguard to lead the *umma*, or global Muslim community, toward the end of jahiliyya and the creation of an Islamic state were heard by many. His words would continue to inspire far beyond his death, and *Milestones'* literal and unyielding interpretations of the sacred texts of Islam, and of the *Salaf*, still resonate in contemporary Islamist literature. West Point's Combating Terrorism Center conducted a wide-ranging survey of Salafi literature that found that Sayyid Qutb was among the most prominent authors in Salafi literature, and was frequently cited by leading contemporary Salafi-jihadi ideologues such as Ayman al-Zawahiri and Abu Muhammad al-Maqdisi.[5]

After Sayyid Qutb's execution, his brother Muhammad became one of his most vigorous and vociferous advocates. Muhammad was born in 1915 in the same town as his elder brother, the second of five siblings.[6] He lived with Sayyid, their two sisters, and their mother in Helwan, a suburb of Cairo, during the late 1920s. He was arrested in July 1965 for alleged participation in his brother's intended plot to overthrow the Egyptian government and replace it with an Islamic state. He was eventually released from prison, in 1972, and found safe haven with his fellow members of the Muslim Brotherhood in Saudi Arabia, where he edited and published his brother's books.[7] He was always studious and determined, but lived largely in his younger brother's shadow. Following his brother's death in 1966, Muhammad published widely in defense of Sayyid's positions, and his positive contributions to the reform movement and to Muslims generally, from a great many detractors who had criticized Qutb's arguments and incendiary messages. In 1975 Muhammad published a lengthy letter in *al-Shihab,* the periodical of the Lebanese Muslim Brotherhood, writing, "I myself heard him [Sayyid] say more than once: 'We are preachers and not judges. Our objective is not to legislate against people, but to teach them this truth: that there is no god but God. The fact is that people do not understand what this formula requires of them.'"[8] In *Muslim Extremism in Egypt,* Gilles Kepel writes that Muhammad Qutb sought to steer his brother's thought between two sides of the spectrum: on the one hand, "extremists" like Shukri Mustafa's Takfir wa'l-Hijra, who advocated a complete withdrawal from the ignorance of modern society, and on the other hand the "ultra-moderates," like Hasan al-Hudaybi (the appointed leader of the Muslim Brotherhood after al-Banna's death, and a rival to Qutb), who critiqued Qutb's message in his book *Preachers, Not Judges,* (*Du'at la Qudat*).[9] After the time that Usama bin Ladin entered King 'Abd al-'Aziz University in Jeddah in 1976, he began attending lectures by Muhammad Qutb. Each week, Sayyid's younger brother would lecture at the university, where many of the professors were members of the Brotherhood and Bin Ladin and the other students were well versed in the elder Qutb's *Milestones* and *In the Shade of the Qur'an.*[10] Qutb was widely popular with the student body and his continuance of Sayyid's message of action and organization in order to implement Allah's rule on earth were well received in the Salafi circles of Saudi Arabia in the 1970s. He is still residing in Mecca at the time of writing, nearing ninety-five years of age.

QUTB'S MESSAGE

Sayyid Qutb urged Muslims to consider that violent jihad was necessary in order to bring about *hakimiyyat Allah* (God's rule on earth), "an imperative that all Muslims must strive to implement or impose immediately."[11] Qutb also maintained that, because the Muslim world is governed according to secular laws (*ahkam al-kuffar*), it is then under the rule of *Dar al-Harb* (the land of war), and outside the abode of Islam. Jihad against the apostate rulers of these states, Qutb argued, was just according to the *Shari`a*. Furthermore, he stated that participation in this jihad was an obligation for every Muslim. Those who refused to contribute were deemed apostates, which makes their bloodshed licit in combat operations. This line of argument would have significant ramifications on the individuals he influenced—not only Usama bin Ladin, but his entire generation of activist Muslims.

Qutb's *Fi Zilal al-Qur'an (In the Shade of the Qur'an)*, written during his imprisonment in the late 1950s, is one of the most influential twentieth-century commentaries on the Qur'an. In *Milestones,* his seminal work, Sayyid Qutb argues that mankind has become morally bankrupt, that new leadership is required, and that Islam should be the way of life and code of law for, ultimately, all of mankind. Notions like democracy, socialism, and nationalism all fail in the end, but now is the time for Islam to emerge. In that book, he also states that the Qur'an was inspired in phases to adapt to the needs of society. Clearly, this view would seem to validate an interpretive approach to doctrine (and a radical departure from the views of early Salafi reformers in Arabia two centuries earlier). This very principle was a clear engagement with modernity, in fact meeting it on its own terms, and allowing Muslims to institute governments ruled by the Shari`a that adopt to the contemporary society. In this discussion, Qutb invokes the term *takhalluf,* or backwardness—a loaded term for Arabs if there ever was one, denoting the decline and state of decay of the contemporary Arab society in which he lived. For Qutb, Islam has no nation or race, as it regards all mankind as equal and deserving of social justice.[12] Qutb also states, it should be noted, that the greatest jihad is that of the self against treacherous desires and the continual struggle to truly act in the interest of the community of Muslims. In his 1951 book entitled, *Al-Salam al-'Alami wa'l-Islam* (Global Peace and Islam), Qutb predicts that Islam would eventually be engaged in a global war with the United States.[13] Qutb went further to say that the United States has pursued war in the name of peace, and there will come a time when Muslim oil and industry will fuel American economic exploitation.

FROM THE TREE OF QUTB

Born in India three years before Sayyid Qutb, Abu'l-A'la Mawdudi (1903–1979) worked much along the same track as his Egyptian contemporary, attempting to elucidate the meaning of jihad in the society in which he lived. He worked in the then-princely state of Hyderabad as a journalist for the first seven years of his professional career, when he left to pursue his own writing with *Jihad in Islam* (al-jihad fi'l-Islam), published in 1927.[14] He went on to write dozens of books, covering Islamic topics and addressing contemporary issues with a modern style and approach. In *Jihad for the Sake of God* (al-Jihad fi sabil Allah) he explores the concept of jihad extensively, as well as the concept of war from a Western perspective. It is a work of modern literature, relying on reasoning rather than citations from classical Islamic sources and scholars to make its arguments.[15] Mawdudi argues that Islam is a revolutionary social movement that aims to establish social justice and that jihad is the method through which it is achieved. He goes on to say that the call to Islam is, then, one to end tyranny and install a system of equity, in the interests of social justice. Curiously, the text relies on modern philosophy, seemingly a direct antecedent of what al-Afghani propounded a generation earlier. Mawdudi's legacy is not, to be more precise, a branch from Qutb's teachings, but a separate entity, intertwined through the decades by a similarity of ideas rather than direct involvement or cooperation.

In 1941 Mawdudi founded *Jamaat-i-Islami* (Islamic Group) and served as president of the organization until 1972. In 1947 he moved to newly emerging Pakistan and worked toward the establishment of an Islamic state. He was arrested and imprisoned multiple times; his 1953 fatwa (or legal edict) declaring the Ahmadiyya movement to be apostate resulted in Mawdudi receiving a death sentence from a military court in

Pakistan, although it was ultimately commuted to life imprisonment, a term of which he only served two years.[16] His movement was banned in 1958 amid martial law, but is still active in Bangladesh, with branches in the United Kingdom that undertake extensive youth activities, including the U.K. Islamic Mission and the Islamic Foundation.[17] Ironically he died in the United States in 1979, where he came in search of medical treatment. Mawdudi's Jamaat-i-Islami had a great influence on jihadi groups in Afghanistan in the 1970s, and on groups like the Hofstad Network in the Netherlands, who translated the works of Qutb and Mawdudi into Dutch.

Mawdudi argued that the responsibility for the negative situation of the umma lay with the rulers who claimed to be Muslim but were not sincere in their faith; they did not adhere to the right course of action on behalf of the interests of the community. Thus, he concluded that these Muslim rulers were apostates and needed to be fought with the sword— along the same lines that Ibn Taymiyya had declared the nominally Muslim Mongol rulers as apostate in order to justify a war against them six centuries earlier. The end goal for his Jamaat-i-Islami was to usher in an Islamic state, which Mawdudi dubbed a "theo-democracy." Clearly, Mawdudi, like Qutb, had engaged in numerous innovations—new rulings of significance, loosely in the name of Salafism, that had little real basis or justification in Islamic doctrine.

These innovations did not go undetected by the Salafi establishment of Saudi Arabia, still believing itself to be the sole claimant to the mantle of "Salafi" and the official clerics of Mecca and Medina. The models of Qutb and Mawdudi presented serious and immediate threats to the rulers of Muslim countries; their agitations in print were palpable on the ground in many countries; where groups of Muslims were organizing and demanding their version of Islamic rule. This threat has been particularly menacing to Saudi Arabia, where in 1979, Juhayman al-'Utaybi, a fiery young militant Salafi activist, and a group of his followers laid siege to the Grand Mosque in Mecca and held it captive until a group of French Legionnaires (who had converted to Islam in order to enter the sanctuary), gassed al-'Utaybi's men out of underground tunnels beneath the Ka'aba.[18] Al-'Utaybi has studied under the Saudi *ulama'* (scholars) and his revolt against the establishment was felt strongly. By the 1980s, and especially in the 1990s, the Saudis funded an all-out information campaign to re-take Salafism.

This campaign is still ongoing, and can be seen prominently in the online literature they produce and promote. On one of the Saudi Salafi establishment's network of websites, Salafipublications.com, Qutb and Mawdudi are viewed as dangerous, heretical revolutionaries that are ob-sessed with overthrowing rulers. The article, entitled "Abu A'laa Mawdudi, Qutb and the Prophets of Allaah," attacks Qutb and Mawdudi's modern-ist, audacious criticism of the prophets and admonishes their "danger-ous" tactics:

> This [Joseph's request to become Custodian in Egypt] was not a de-mand to be the Minister of Finance only, as some people understand, this was not a demand of the ministerial office of finance only, but a demand for dictatorship. As a result this position which Sayyidina Yusuf [Joseph] got is almost the same which Mussolini enjoyed in Italy in these days. (Tafhimat, Part II, 5th ed.)

And Mawdudi has also spoken about Yunus [Jonah] and Adam in oth-er places with similar words of belittlement and presumption:

> Have you O Sunni, seen a verse in the Qur'an, or a hadith of the Mes-senger (salla Allah 'alayhi wa'sallam [peace and blessings be upon him]), or a saying of the Sahaba [companions of the Prophet], or of the Imams after them, or of the Scholars of Ahl us-Sunna [People of the Sunna] throughout the ages, in which such mannerisms have been adopted to those upon whom Allah's speech was revealed and in whose hearts it settled?! [19]

Blasphemies against the prophets are a serious sin (Islam recognizes prophets and messengers beginning with Adam, until the Prophet Mu-hammad). The Saudi establishment went so far as to excommunicate Mawdudi, Qutb and their followers from Islam.

> And these words are words of kufr [disbelief] and apostasy as has been said by the People of Knowledge, such as Imam Ibn Baz [Bin Baz] and others. And this is indeed the end-result of all the callers

to the innovated Hakimiyya [rule] of the Kharijites [an early sect that split away from the Islamic community]. They revile the Prophets and Messengers on purely political and leadership grounds, then they revile the Companions of Allah's Messenger [as occurred from both Qutb and Mawdudi] and then those who are poisoned with their teachings and influenced by their destructive thought, their followers and loyalists, revile the Inheritors of the Prophets, the Scholars. So they call them "the scholars of women's menses and impurities," "present in body, absent in mind," "forced to make flattery," and other such repugnant slanders and lies, the objective of which is to make the Scholars of Salafiyya to fall and so that the callers to Revolution and Qutbiyya [Qutbism] may rise and stretch their necks.

In summary, this is the Hakimiyya of the Activists and all those groups to whom Leadership, Imamate [an Islamic government under an Imam] and Hakimiyya is the overall concern, then they are all upon the thought of Mawdudi, by the route of Sayyid Qutb. And it was Mawdudi who coined the phrase al-Hakimiyya, and it was unknown to the Salaf. So know the chains of narration of the Innovators.[20]

This passage exemplifies the extreme to which infighting among these rival groups had reached, in essence each side labeling the other a nonbeliever and a potential enemy in combat. This Salafi establishment in Saudi Arabia included an international network funded by petro-dollars to propagate the doctrine of the Salafi clerics of the Kingdom. Keenly, those clerics accuse those who seek to overthrow their Muslim rulers or advocate political resistance to be outside the tolerable bounds of Islam according to their interpretations of the early texts, and the lives of the Salaf. But for Qutb, Mawdudi, and their predecessors such as al-Zawahiri and Bin Ladin, these Saudi Salafis were merely puppets who enjoyed their place of power solely because of Western support. Clearly, by the late 1990s, these debates were globalized via the Internet; but three decades earlier Salafi activism was establishing itself in the United States.

BEGINNINGS OF ISLAMIST ACTIVISM IN AMERICA
Without doubt, Islamist activism in the United States was influenced by the contending currents of self-proclaimed "Salafi" scholars and the followers of Qutb, Mawdudi, and other reformers in their ilk. Yet, Islamic

activism in the United States is diverse, and within the scope of Muslim activism, there is a range of Salafi activism, as seen in the preceding chapter. In some of these latter groups, foreign Islamist educational and ideological influences are manifest in an agenda focused on the problems facing the global Muslim community, with an emphasis on Palestine, Iraq, and Afghanistan. These currents, streaming from the Islamic revivalist movements of the Middle East, continue to shape the debate among Muslims in America. Perhaps the most pertinent example is that of the Muslim Brotherhood. The Brotherhood has operated in the United States since the early 1960s, then primarily through student and youth activist organizations. The first chapter of the Brotherhood was founded in the Midwest, and incorporated as a "cultural society."[21] Today, ties are weak between the *al-Ikhwan al-Muslimun* in Egypt and Muslim organizations founded in the United States in the sixties, but the Brotherhood's ideals now mobilize a contemporary generation of American Muslims along Islamic reform principles established a century earlier.

Islamist activism in the United States began in earnest with the formation of the Muslim Students Association (MSA) at the University of Illinois Urbana-Champaign in 1963. Three of the MSA's founders were members of the Muslim Brotherhood: Dr. Ahmad Sakr, Dr. Ahmad Totonji, and Jamal Barzinji, who helped bring the teachings of the Brotherhood, those of Hasan al-Banna and Sayyid Qutb, to Muslim students.[22] Out of this original group of activists sprang the most influential Muslim organizations: the Islamic Society of North America (ISNA), the Islamic Circle of North America (ICNA), and others. These organizations were among the first to provide English-language materials on Islam to Muslims and non-Muslims alike, and gained an early footing among the Muslim community in America.

One of the leaders of the early Brotherhood movement in America was Ahmed Elkadi, an Egyptian-born surgeon and former personal physician to King Faisal of Saudi Arabia. He headed the group in the U.S. from 1984 to 1994 and went public with his past in 2004.[23] He says the Brotherhood was successful in helping establish mosques and Islamic organizations in the 1990s, which were partly funded by the Saudi government, who shared in their endeavors to spread this version of Islam in the United States. Additionally, Elkadi participated in the creation of the

Muslim Youth of North America, an organization that attempted to recruit high school students to Islam by sponsoring soccer events and offering scholarships, as well as a line of clothing. Highly active, Elkadi also served as president of the North American Islamic Trust (NAIT), a group created by the MSA in Indiana in 1973 that owns over 300 titles to mosques in the United States and Canada.[24] MSA members also formed ISNA, one of the oldest and largest Muslim organizations in America.

Since the early days of Muslim activism in America, the original organizations have branched out and in many ways the influence of the Brotherhood has been much diluted. In addition, there are, to some extent, indigenous Muslim civic organizations that have arisen since the 1960s. While some share doctrinal standards with similarities to Salafism, they choose to partake in the democratic process and affect change through nonviolent means. At the same time, it should be cautioned that those which instill a rigid Salafi mindset into young or new Muslims leave them vulnerable to the influence of more radical elements that reject any law or political effort other than the Shari'a.

The Muslim American Society (MAS) can be seen as an American offshoot of the Brotherhood established in the sixties. MAS is perhaps the foremost Islamist organization attempting to fulfill the objectives of the Muslim Brotherhood in the United States, but with an American agenda.[25] A top MAS leader, Shaker Elsayed, acknowledged, "Ikhwan [Brotherhood] members founded MAS, but MAS went way beyond that point of conception."[26] The MAS now operates an activist wing, an Islamic university, a council of Islamic schools in the United States, a magazine, a youth mission, and offers fatwas from Imam Muhammad al-Hanooti, a Palestinian-born Mufti trained at al-Azhar University in Cairo who is also accused of raising more than $6 million for Hamas.[27] Imam al-Hanooti was investigated in the 1993 World Trade Center bombings when he was imam of the New Jersey mosque where now-imprisoned cleric 'Umar 'Abd al-Rahman (better known as "the blind shaykh") often delivered speeches. A member of the congregation from that mosque, Mohammed Salameh, drove the rented van and detonated the explosives in the World Trade Center on February 26, 1993. MAS, however, is focused primarily on education, with programs for training teachers and designing curriculum, as well as the Islamic

American University, a chiefly online school with an office near Detroit, Michigan, and extensive youth programs.

In its mission statement, MAS claims:

> The Muslim American Society (MAS) traces its historical roots back to the call of the Prophet Muhammad (Peace be upon him). Its more recent roots, however, can be traced to the Islamic revival movement which evolved at the turn of the twentieth century.
>
> This movement brought the call of Islam to Muslims throughout the globe to reestablish Islam as a total way of life. The call and the spirit of the movement reached the shores of North America with arrival of Muslim students and immigrants in the late 1950s and early 1960s.[28]

The twentieth-century movement described is the Muslim Brotherhood, and these early North American Muslim organizations were among the earliest publishers of the movement's key literature, such as Qutb's *Milestones* and *In the Shade of the Qur'an*. Their mission goes on to state, "These early pioneers and Islamic movement followers established in 1963 the Muslim Student Association (MSA) of the United States and Canada as a rallying point in their endeavor to serve Islam and Muslims in North America. Other services and outreach organizations soon followed, such as the North American Islamic Trust (NAIT), the Islamic Medical Association (IMA), the Muslim Arab Youth Association (MAYA) and the Muslim Youth of North America (MYNA), to name a few." These organizations clearly laid the groundwork for MAS, as well as a number of other Islamic advocacy organizations.

One other such example is the Islamic Circle of North America (ICNA), which describes itself as a grassroots Islamic organization working toward the "establishment of Islam in all spheres of life" in America and worldwide. ICNA is located in Jamaica, New York, and was founded in 1971, also by former MSA members. They also host a popular website entitled "whyislam"[29] and offer *usul al-fiqh* (methods of Islamic jurisprudence), Arabic language, *fatwa* (legal rulings), and other services. ICNA also operates "Young Muslims" websites; under the "books" section of the website, titles by Hasan al-Banna and Abu al-A'la Mawdudi are provided among the suggested reading.[30]

Through some of the leading organizations discussed here, two branches of the Salafi movement (namely, those of Egypt and Saudi Arabia) have exercised a great deal of influence over the American Muslim community. There is no doubt these ideologies moderated as a result of being transplanted to the United States, turning to civic methods of activism to achieve their goals. But beyond the mainstream organizing activities, where violence is condemned, the curriculum of Salafi leaders has been instilled upon countless American Muslims, and some of that curriculum includes the notions of Islamist reform and revival that are shared by jihadists. Nonetheless, the impact of foreign ideological currents and their interests are felt throughout the community, in its mosques, political, social, and educational institutions.

The plethora of American activist organizations—MSA, ISNA, ICNA, MAS, et al.—that had evolved out of the work done by the first generation of Brotherhood emissaries were not advocates of violent hostility against the United States; they were contending for educational and ideological influence over the Muslim community in America. In a number of ways, these groups play an important social function in providing an interlocutor for American Muslims. Although it could be argued that these groups have injected the Muslim community with Salafi influences, the major Islamic advocacy organizations have opposed militancy toward the United States and have increasingly tried to address the question of what it means to be Muslim in America today. This debate clearly needs to take place on a larger stage, so that the Muslim community can have a meaningful dialogue with their fellow Americans, but also understand where 'Salafi' and 'Islamist' elements can be healthy political actors.

While the emissaries of Salafism—mostly in the form of Muslim Brotherhood alumni—took to organizing the Muslim community in America in the 1970s, a much more virulent strand of Salafi activism was burgeoning in the Middle East. Also members of the Muslim Brotherhood, Salafis in Jordan and Egypt were more aggressive in their stance against tyrannical governments and the need to overthrow them with force. Much of this Salafi activism was driven by the humiliation of Muslim defeat at the hands of Israel, and the Arabs' disgraceful capitulation. These Islamists were still, in the long term, seeking to supplant the rule of law with their interpretation of the Shari'a, but they had the more immediate goal of redress for the shameful state of affairs in which the Islamic world was

languishing. But as campaigns against Arab governments yielded little
fruit for the Islamists, leaders like Abdullah 'Azzam found a battlefield in
Afghanistan on which to act out the next chapter of Islamist resistance,
and a galvanized Salafi-jihadi movement forged out of the war against
Soviet occupation beginning in 1979.

Four

THE TRIUMPH OF ISLAM OVER GODLESSNESS

"Indeed Islamic history is not written except with the blood of Martyrs"
—*Abdullah `Azzam*

IN JULY 2008 THE AUTHOR found himself in a somewhat heated debate in an otherwise sleepy setting at the University of Otago, in Dunedin, New Zealand. After presenting a lecture on the evolution of the Salafi-jihadi movement, I was confronted by a politely resolute Professor Najibullah Lafraie, who, after serving as Afghan Foreign Minister from 1992 to 1996, received asylum in New Zealand and came to teach at the university. He was obstinate in his position that Abdullah `Azzam was a national hero for the Afghan people, and a liberator. Lafraie fought alongside many of his countrymen in the battle against the Soviet occupation of Afghanistan from 1979 to 1989, and also knew `Azzam personally. He felt insulted by an insinuation of the late `Azzam's legacy with bin Ladin or al-Qa`ida. Although that sentiment is felt by many other non-Salafi Muslims engaged, to one extent or the other, in the Afghanistan struggle against the Soviets, `Azzam nonetheless served as a spiritual guide and war hero for the generation of Salafists that went on to attack Washington and New York in September 2001—and plotted and attempted numerous other operations.[1]

`Azzam was assassinated on November 24, 1989, at the end of the same year the Soviets withdrew from Afghanistan in defeat. `Azzam was driving with two of his sons, Ibrahim and Muhammad, as three bombs

detonated along the road as they arrived at a mosque on a Friday in Peshawar, in western Pakistan.[2] The blast reportedly sent some of the bodies
flying 100 meters, killing `Azzam and his two sons. The party responsible
for the assassination is still unknown; suspects include rival Afghan mi-
litias, bin Ladin himself, and intelligence agencies, but none can be sub-
stantiated.[3] `Azzam's legacy is epitomized in an Islamist biography online:

> May Allah accept him as a martyr, and grant him the highest station
> in Paradise. The struggle which he stood for continues, despite the
> enemies of Islam. There is not a Land of Jihad today in the world,
> nor a Mujahid fighting in Allah's Way, who is not inspired by the life,
> teachings and works of Shaykh Abdullah `Azzam (May Allah have
> Mercy on him).[4]

Abdullah was born under the British Mandate of Palestine in 1941,
in a small village in the province of Jenin. He was known as a pious child
who took his schoolwork seriously and taught fellow school children les-
sons from Islam. He was an avid teacher of Islam his entire life, from the
time he began teaching in Adder in southern Jordan, until his death in
Peshawar. He received a BA in Islamic Law from Damascus University
in 1966, not long before Sayyid Qutb was assassinated. He emigrated to
Jordan after the Israeli capture of the West Bank in 1967, outraged by
the general lack of resistance from his fellow Palestinians and Muslims.
He resolved to join the jihad, and spent a year and a half contributing to
the struggle for Palestinian liberation before he decided to move to Egypt
to further his higher education at al-Azhar University. During his stay
in Egypt he became acquainted with the family of Sayyid Qutb, and the
future generation of Egyptian ideologues of jihad, `Umar `Abd al-Rahman
and Ayman al-Zawahiri.[5] By 1973 `Azzam had earned a Master's and PhD
in the Principles of Islamic Jurisprudence (*Usul al-Fiqh*) from that university, the oldest and most acclaimed in the Sunni Muslim world.[6] His
scholarly credentials reflected the primacy `Azzam placed on Islamic
scholarship in the context of jihadi activism. It would also drive a wedge
between himself and many of the more secular elements that drove the
Palestinian resistance throughout the 1970s.

In the late 1970s, 'Azzam was offered a teaching job at King 'Abd al-'Aziz University in Jeddah, one of the premier Saudi Salafi educational institutions, where a young Usama bin Ladin was among the students he taught. 'Azzam had apparently been relieved to leave the jihadist scene in Palestine, to which he had returned in 1973 after his advanced studies in Egypt, as the secular flavor of the Palestine Liberation Organization (PLO) and other organized pro-Palestinian movements were contrary to his mission. In 1979 he left his teaching position in Jeddah after hearing news of the emerging jihad against the Soviet Union in Afghanistan.[7] 'Azzam was a lecturer briefly at the International Islamic University in Islamabad, Pakistan, before he became immersed in the jihadi resistance scene and dedicated himself to the effort full time. He then moved to Peshawar to assist in the grand effort of recruiting and organizing Muslim, primarily Arab, fighters to join the jihad. The call to jihad 'Azzam preached was the first occasion in the modern history of the Salafi movement in which Salafi activists were actually training and organizing the Muslims they called to jihad, rather than urging them to action in a general sense. It was also the first military battle zone the Salafis entered since the Wahhabi-Sa'udi forces fought to gain control of Mecca and Medina, roughly two centuries earlier. The ultimate victory of these mujahidin elevated the concept and act of jihad among a great many Salafis, and it would remain the issue around which the movement would focus until the present.

'Azzam was often acclaimed for his oratorical skill and charisma. During his decade in Pakistan and Afghanistan engaged in the jihad, 'Azzam gave hundreds of lectures and wrote a number of pieces on jihad, the books *Join the Caravan* and *In Defense of Muslim Lands* carried his message of a vibrant jihad movement awakening the umma to an audience outside the personal, informal setting of his regular lectures or his oratory from the pulpit. His activism, though, transcended the realm of activism; among his influential accomplishments was overseeing the establishment of *Bayt al-Ansar,* "House of Supporters" (of the jihad effort), and *Maktab al-Khidmat,* the "Mujahidin's Services Bureau," where Bin Ladin first became involved in the Afghan jihad, providing funding and assisting in the organizing effort.

Al-Qa'ida grew out of the organizational activities of Usama bin Ladin in Pakistan and Afghanistan beginning in 1980. After moving to Peshawar,

Bin Ladin began organizing a guesthouse for incoming foreign mujahidin, the Bayt al-Ansar. Under Abdullah 'Azzam, he also published *Jihad* magazine, one of the first periodicals to be devoted to this modern notion of *jihadi* militancy outside of the sponsorship of the state or official institutions. These endeavors evolved into Maktab al-Khidmat, established in 1984 for mujahidin arriving to join the fight. 'Azzam preached jihad as a moral and individual obligation for all Muslims. Through this organization, he and Bin Ladin recruited, equipped, trained, and indoctrinated formative mujahidin and came to see them as a foundation for global efforts after the Afghan jihad.

But it was 'Azzam's ideology, built on the centuries of Salafi reform, that allowed him to consolidate a plan of action and act it out on the international stage—more so than anyone before him had done. The impact of the mujahidin's ultimate victory over the godlessness which the Soviet Union sought to impose, and the strength of the coherent doctrine of jihad that came out of it, were quite clearly the drivers that created the jihadist offensive of the 1990s that culminated in 9/11. The most potent of these ideas was that jihad must be waged—as a sixth pillar of Islam—in every land where Muslims once ruled and unbelievers—either nonbelievers or hypocritical, secular Arab regimes—had claimed power. He was clear: Afghanistan was only the beginning. The list for action following the Afghan campaign in Palestine (the reclamation of Jerusalem was of utmost concern), included the Philippines, Syria, Lebanon, Chad, Egypt, South Yemen, and Soviet Uzbekistan.[8] South Yemen and Uzbekistan were clearly extensions of Soviet rule over, or at least subjugation of, Muslim lands similar to Afghanistan. But the political situations in the other countries mentioned were more nuanced, and could be extended to essentially any country with a Muslim heritage that was now in need of Salafi liberation. It was the problem of wounded Islam the world over, he told Muslims, and jihad by the rifle was the solution. Moreover, the primary goal of these military campaigns was the establishment of an Islamic state, the *Khilafa*.

For Salafi doctrine, 'Azzam introduced a critical principle. Although Qutb and others before him had raised it, 'Azzam seemed to solidify the notion that rule by any law other than what Allah revealed through the Qur'an and the sayings of His Prophet was illicit, and Muslims should rightfully revolt against it. Clearly, this edict applied to every government in the Muslim world. This argument—over the nature of the law and the necessary place of the Shari`a in it—has been a pivotal one for Salafis over the past two decades.[9] Potentially, this determination could put anyone who supports such "man-made" laws (including those who vote in democratic elections or pay taxes to secular regimes) outside the pale of Islam, making them an unbeliever and a legal target in war. This principle has legitimized terrorist acts and the killing of civilians for a great many Salafi-oriented groups.

By the time of his martyrdom in 1989, Abdullah `Azzam had solidified a powerful and cohesive message: jihad is your obligation as a Muslim, and a score of countries are in need of Islamic liberation (or re-conquest, as it were). In spreading this message, and sacrificing his life to it, `Azzam laid out a roadmap for redirecting Muslim anger and humiliation at their status in the world and the wretched condition of the Arab World, offering an opportunity for young men to fight for the betterment of their fellow Muslims. His list of countries for future jihad was altered, slightly, for the coming decade's political reality by the leading Salafi thinkers of the time. The break-up of the Soviet Union in 1991 ushered in numerous opportunities for militants in Central Asia, but that was to prove the northeastern frontier of jihad and few Arab fighters played any critical role in Islamist movements in Uzbekistan or other former–Soviet Union (FSU) countries. In Southeast Asia, meanwhile, there was support and cooperation between Arab Salafi militants and their burgeoning counterparts in the region. As Olivier Roy quite accurately put it: radicalized Muslims "are fighting at the frontiers of their imaginary *ummah.*" Throughout the decade, jihadists organized and fought campaigns, to differing extents, in Somalia, Bosnia, Kosovo, Chechnya, Afghanistan, Kashmir, the Philippines and Indonesia, and lastly Kenya and Tanzania. But while active (in large part thanks to Saudi petrodollars, as we see in chapter six), the movement lacked a clear successor to `Azzam, who would take up the mantle of Islamic resistance and renewal under the standard of the *Salafiyya.* Numerous clerics and veteran fighters alike vied to fill that void after 1989, most of whom had come up in the post-Qutb era, implicitly accepting the necessity of armed struggle in order to implement divine law in ailing Muslim society.

■ ■ ■

The al-Kifah Refugee Center first opened its offices in a humble apart-
ment on Atlantic Avenue in Brooklyn in 1986, with little more than a desk,
a phone, and a fax machine.[10] The Boerum Hill neighborhood of Brooklyn
has long been a destination for Arab and Muslim immigrants. Al-Kifah
began within the al-Farooq Mosque on the same street to raise money and
provide recruits for the mujahidin in Afghanistan. The mosque was a hot-
bed of activity in the late 1980s and early 1990s. 'Umar 'Abd al-Rahman,
the blind shaykh serving a life sentence in a New York prison for his role
in the 1993 World Trade Center bombing, arrived in Brooklyn in 1990
and was a regular speaker at the al-Farooq Mosque. But throughout the
anti-Soviet jihad, the mujahidin had the support of the United States government, and al-Kifah itself has a number of ties to the CIA that have never fully been disclosed. The Brooklyn al-Kifah center did indeed feature
CIA-sponsored lecturers, as well as provide training in automatic rifles by
instructors from the National Rifle Association, martial arts classes, and
other instructional courses for the aspiring mujahid.[11]

Abdullah 'Azzam traveled to the United States on a number of occasions to raise funds and support for the jihad. In 1988 he preached his
fiery message to crowded mosques in New York and New Jersey—one of
them being the al-Farooq Mosque in Brooklyn. He solicited donations—
many in the form of checks made out to his personal U.S. bank account—
while calling for a revolution that would "ignite the spark that may one
day burn Western interests all over the world."[12] In fact, the lines between
al-Kifah and 'Azzam's Maktab al-Khidmat (once again, the precursor
organization to al-Qa'ida in Peshawar) become blurred; both organizations are vehicles for advancing the cause of jihad under overlapping
leadership.

Al-Kifah drew supporters far beyond its immigrant neighborhood
in Brooklyn. An open letter from the Islamic Society of North America
(ISNA) dated August 8, 1991, endorses the work of al-Kifah Refugee Center, stating, "We urge you to support them and to contribute to their project in order that they may do their part in accomplishing our mission
of raising the Word of Allah to the Highest."[13] The English translation of
the Arabic text reads "Alkifah Refugee Center" and its mailing address as

"Maktab al-Khidmat al-Mujahidin, P.O. Box 294, Brooklyn, New York." It appears that in the public record even, al-Kifah and Maktab al-Khidmat are interchangeable.

Al-Kifah's efforts were embraced by the Muslim-American community, through which hundreds of thousands of dollars made their way to the mujahidin in Afghanistan. Of course, that is trivial in comparison to the $500 million sent annually by the government of the United States and Saudi Arabia.[14] Although its offices in Brooklyn closed after the 1993 World Trade Center bombing, a number of other branches (or more accurately, 'jihad' offices tied to 'Azzam's efforts) had been operating in the United States. Perhaps the most prominent of these was the Boston office, which later changed its name to Care International. The Boston office published an English translation of 'Azzam's *Join the Caravan,* and a newsletter called *al-Hussam* (the Sword), which positioned itself an authentic source of information on "jihad action."[15] The founders of Care International were eventually convicted of tax fraud in January 2008, following investigations into their support for jihadi activities.

The confluence of United States and jihadi interests ended after the Soviets withdrew from Afghanistan in 1989. It is here where the legacy of 'Azzam was picked up by thinkers like Abu Muhammad al-Maqdisi, and the organizational structure created in the 1980s was repurposed for other jihadist campaigns. These would of course turn against the United States by the late 1990s, a point forcefully made with the 1998 U.S. Embassy bombings in Kenya and Tanzania.

■ ■ ■

Salafi literature began arriving on the Internet in the mid-1990s. This medium introduced the writings of 'Abd Allah 'Azzam, Sayyid Qutb, and other late revolutionary Islamist leaders, as well as contemporary Salafi ideologues like Abu Muhammad al-Maqdisi and Abu Basir al-Tartusi, to a new generation of young Muslims. This took place largely through the initial efforts of the Afghan veterans from the 1970s and their sympathizers and supporters, who continued to globalize the jihadi movement toward an Islamic awakening.

Abu Muhammad al-Maqdisi is one of today's most influential Salafi thinkers.[16] In his prolific writings, the Jordanian scholar—best known to the West as the mentor of the butchering Abu Mus'ab al-Zarqawi, head of the early al-Qa'ida group in Iraq who was killed in June 2006—reiterated many of 'Azzam's themes, in a twenty-first-century setting. Al-Maqdisi, whose full name is 'Assim bin Muhammad bin Tahir al-Barqawi (his honorific al-Maqdisi is derived from Bayt al-Maqdis, a name for Jerusalem), was born in Nablus in 1959.[17] He left the city and moved with his family at age three or four to Kuwait, where he completed his secondary education. His father sent him to study science at the University of Mosul in Iraq, although he would have preferred to study Shari'a law at the Islamic University in Medina. In his early years, while forging his own beliefs and identity, al-Maqdisi says he studied and sat with followers of Sayyid Qutb, members of Juhayman al-'Utaybi's group, and other reformers and jihadis, although he found points of criticism among nearly all of them. He set himself aside as a pure scholar, and would become one of the most influential thinkers of the jihadi movement from the late 1990s onward.

Maqdisi traveled widely between Jordan, Kuwait, Saudi Arabia, Pakistan, and Afghanistan in the late 1980s and early 1990s.[18] He argued that the youth who had fought in Afghanistan in the 1980s, or those who were too young but were inspired by it in later years, lacked the proper religious guidance, and thus were damaging the movement and causing a distraction from its end goals. This explosion of young, energized mujahidin has benefited greatly from the battlefields of Chechnya, Bosnia, and other sites after the Afghan jihad; but in their youthful exuberance, the young mujahidin rush to carry out operations without considering the consequences to the movement or for the umma.[19]

Accordingly, Maqdisi set out to establish a singular, unified doctrine (a challenge that had not yet been achieved in over 200 years of Salafi activism). *Hadhihi 'aqidatuna* (This is Our Doctrine), is one of his most significant works, but also arguably one of the more influential, and controversial, in Salafism today. It is a bold refutation against those who subordinate divine law to secular law, and those who subject religion to the "whims of the tyrants and crusaders." Obedience to secular laws written by disbelievers is sinful—Muslims must always prioritize Islamic principles and strive to live by the Shari'a. Authority and obedience are due to rightly guided leadership, and it is an obligation for Muslims to resist tyrants, dictators, and anyone opposed to the establishment of Islamic law, he writes.[20]

Maqdisi sets out to make clear in his writing that his understanding of Islam is entirely incompatible with the notion of government by the people.[21] Moreover, he argues that a state of discord will reign on earth until the laws governing man are returned to God. He applies this model to virtually every country of interest; clearly the United States epitomizes this blasphemous model of governance, but among all Arab and Muslim countries, he focuses much of his criticism on Saudi Arabia.[22] Maqdisi's choice to attack the Saudi state and its establishment Salafi clerics is clearly intentional—those ruling over Mecca and Medina have enjoyed tremendous legitimacy in the Muslim world as a de facto authority in Islam. Maqdisi seeks to undercut this authority, but also makes explicitly clear that he is, at heart, a *Najdi* (one from the Najd, or eastern Arabia—where Wahhabism originated). Again, one sees how critical ideological legitimacy is in Muslim society, the world of political and religious activism in particular.

One of the most binding and effectual concepts in Salafi-jihadi literature is that of al-Wala' wa'l-Bara,' or love and hate for the sake of Allah. In practice this term refers to loyalty or allegiance to the believers, and enmity toward nonbelievers, in an absolute fashion. At the state level, it meant that those regimes that do not rule by the Shari'a are harboring disbelief—enemies of Allah—and must be confronted. During his travels to Afghanistan at the end of the Soviet campaign in 1989, Maqdisi applied the concept of *al-Wala' wa'l-Bara'* to the Saudi state, publishing *al-Kawashif al-jaliyya fi kufr al-dawla al-Sa'udiyya* (Illuminating Evidence of the Disbelief of the Saudi State).[23] This attack was a significant turn against the Saudis, who had in many ways—primarily financially—been supporters of jihadi campaigns including that against the Soviet Union in Afghanistan. Like Rashid Rida before him, Maqdisi was attempting to bridge the original Wahhabi movement and its doctrine with contemporary Salafism.

MAQDISI: BETWEEN 'AZZAM AND IBN 'ABD AL-WAHHAB

Al-Maqdisi, along with his contemporary militant Salafi scholars, consistently refers to the rulers of Arab regimes as tyrants, saying they rule by their own law, not that of Allah. Even in contemporary critiques, such as those that he makes against the Kuwaiti government, he relies heavily on the writings of Ibn 'Abd al-Wahhab and Ibn Taymiyya; Islam of the past, for Salafis, is always purer than the present.[24] In one of his tracts, entitled "Unveiling the Law of the Jungle" (referring to the laws governing Kuwait in this case), he describes himself as a "pure Najdi Sunni Muslim Arab." This nomenclature is fascinating. It is not enough to present oneself as a Sunni, but it is necessary to also state he is an Arab, and lastly a *Najdi,* or the lineage of Muhammad Ibn 'Abd al-Wahhab circa late eighteenth-century Arabia, one of the prime instigators of this narrative. After Rashid Rida, Ibn 'Abd al-Wahhab's doctrinal tracts become less central to Salafism; with the tumult of Sayyid Qutb's saga, and the redemption tale of 'Azzam's improbable victories against the godless Soviet Union, frenzied activism and violence dominated most Salafi-oriented groups (both violent and nonviolent) until the late 1980s. But scholars like Maqdisi, in the 1990s, began reshaping the ideological landscape toward a unified Salafi doctrine for activism. In doing so, they went back to keystone figures like Ibn 'Abd al-Wahhab and Ibn Taymiyya as the fountainheads of knowledge and spiritual guidance.

In Maqdisi's bid to reclaim the Salafi-Wahhabi lineage, he viciously attacks the present-day rulers of Saudi Arabia. He went so far as to label it *al-dawla al-khabitha,* or the "Evil Nation," and attempted to illustrate how King Fahd was a Freemason, the only logical explanation for his suppression of the Muslim nation at the bequest of his Western masters, and, horrifically, to allow the United States to operate bases in the kingdom. The character of Saudi leaders has not been difficult to criticize, but Maqdisi takes on the bigger challenge of the country's clerical establishment, which calls itself Salafi and condemns the jihadist ideology of Maqdisi and other "Salafi-jihadi" scholars. Maqdisi, repeatedly deriding them as lackeys of their corrupt leaders, says they cannot be trusted, stating quite pointedly that they have sold out their cause for "the riyal, the dollar, and the cross."[25]

Part of Maqdisi and other Muslim clerics' obsession with unity lies in a broader preoccupation with unity in the Arab World. The British scholar Stephen Ulph has described a "Unity Preoccupation"—an absolutist mindset where criticism is perceived as an attack on Arab honor and the prestige of the culture—reflected widely in its media. The writings of key Salafi ideologues like Maqdisi seem to be informed by these cultural tendencies, which persistently call on Muslims to defend the honor of their brothers and sisters in Islam. Throughout the writings of Abu Basir al-Tartusi, Abu Qatada al-Filistini, Ayman al-Zawahiri, and others, there is a persistent theme that Muslims must answer the call to jihad, to avenge the state of humiliating subjugation to which the Islamic world has succumbed.

These trends continue to play out within the United States and across the world, wherever Salafis are organized, as the victory over the Soviets in Afghanistan continues to propel a generation of Islamists now driven more than ever to reclaim their lost heritage and identity.

Five

COVERT ORGANIZING

"According to the official version of history, CIA aid to the Mujahadeen began during 1980, that is to say, after the Soviet army invaded Afghanistan, 24 Dec 1979."[1]

—Zbigniew Brzezinski, National Security Director to Jimmy Carter, 1977 to 1981

THE VICTORY OVER the Godless Soviet superpower was not simply the culmination of battlefield gains for the militant Salafist movement. Rather, it energized a generation of Muslims to see the potential of their strength in the model of Islamic renewal that Abdullah `Azzam offered. That model proved that if Muslims organized themselves and worked together, they could, through divine support, defeat a superpower. But the need for this redemption among the *umma,* in particular the segment of activist Muslims, was rooted in a much broader sense of subjugation and humiliation at the state of Arab culture and the dramatically reduced political standing of Muslims in the twentieth-century world.

Stephen Ulph has described this phenomenon in contemporary Arab and Muslim culture as a preoccupation with nationalism, expressed "through prestige, unity, and tradition." One sees these traits present in a great deal of Salafi literature (and virtually all of that which has been quoted in this book). This is not accidental. Islam has been a great source of honor and prestige for the Arab World, and is seen as being responsible for the advancement of civilization during the Middle Ages, even fueling the European Renaissance. Restoring the lost sense of pride, prestige, and honor among Muslims in relation to their standing in the world is a driving force (or perhaps more accurately a prime selling point) of the rhetoric of Salafi ideologues. They call upon Muslims to join their struggle, to enjoin "pure" Islamic belief and strive toward the creation of a state governed under the Shari'a. But that struggle is framed as one on behalf of the Muslim community, for their honor, and the sanctity of Islam.

Entering a discussion on terrorism in the context of Islamist intellectual development, one could infer that the mass murders carried out in the name of Islam over the past forty years were, in fact, rooted in the Islamic faith. But this discussion, which picked up around 1750, follows the development of the social and political activism that has led to such great violence, distinguishing it from Islam itself. Those currents largely ran counter to the mainstream of Muslim society; Salafi activists have always placed their emphasis on reforming the Muslim community and trying to reshape it around their scriptural interpretations. They saw elements of corruption that had entered Muslim society and that it needed cleansing. During the 1990s the spirit of the mujahidin was rerouted into covert organizing for Salafi reform, paid for through a network of wealthy Saudi financiers, including Usama bin Ladin, who supported volunteer fighters in Muslim conflict zones under the guise of nonprofit charity work.

In February 2003 Enaam Arnaout entered a guilty plea in federal court to a single count of racketeering, for which he received an eleven-year prison sentence, later reduced on appeal to ten years. That charge was for defrauding charitable donors of the Benevolence International Foundation (BIF)—subverting a portion of those funds (around $400,000) for supplies to Bosnian mujahidin without the knowledge of the donors. BIF, however, was part of a much broader network. While Arnaout headed the Illinois office, the organization, funded by Saudi dollars, set up branches across the Muslim world and beyond.[2] Adil Batterjee first met Enaam Arnaout in Peshawar, the meeting place for so many mujahidin in the 1980s. Arnaout had worked for another Saudi charity—in fact BIF's parent organization, the Muslim World League—in his home country of Syria. After Arnaout's brother was killed in 1980 in clashes between the Syrian government and the Muslim Brotherhood, Enaam became involved in Islamist organizing. But his career began modestly; he was a driver assigned to pick up Batterjee from the Islamabad airport and return him to Peshawar, and Batterjee liked his driving style, offering him a job with the nascent charity.[3]

Adil Batterjee held the title of Executive Director of the Benevolence International Foundation, and when the group was designated as a terrorist entity by the United States Treasury Department in late 2002, he was singled out as one of the charity's primary financiers.[4] After Batterjee's official resignation from BIF in 1993, he appointed Enaam Arnaout to head the organization, but records show that Batterjee remained active in the charity, although his involvement was concealed. Regardless of efforts to hide his name from the foundation's official leadership, he—under the guise of charitable work—played a huge role in spreading a form of Salafism focused on jihadi activism, primarily in hot zones of Muslim conflict. Adil Batterjee has never faced justice in an American court for his support for al-Qa'ida. Now in his sixties, he lives in a large walled villa in Jeddah with a golden placard marking his name on the home.[5]

The Batterjee family is well known in the Saudi coastal city of Jeddah, owning an array of businesses, from clinics and pharmacies to an ice cream factory.[6] The city even contains a Batterjee street. More than simply a business family, however, the clan has been politically influential. Adil's uncle, Hisham Nazir (who graduated from the University of California–Berkeley), served as the kingdom's oil minister in the 1990s. Adil seemed to follow in the family mold, earning a degree from the University of Kansas in 1968 in mathematics.[7] After graduation, he returned to Saudi Arabia and joined the fast-growing oil industry. But business was not his passion.

Like many other Muslims around the world, Batterjee was riveted by the 1979 Soviet invasion and occupation of Afghanistan. At first he followed the conflict from Saudi Arabia, but after hearing a moving speech in Mecca, Adil traveled to Pakistan and Afghanistan to a get firsthand experience of the conflict.[8] It was evident he wanted to do everything in his ability to help the mujahidin in fighting the Soviets. In 1987 he founded the predecessor of BIF in Peshawar, Pakistan, the *Lajnat al-Birr al-Islami*, or the Committee for Islamic Benevolence. Batterjee helped train numerous mujahidin, providing them shelter, and even aiding in the movement of troops to the battlefield. The charity quickly rose to become

one of the most prominent and effective in the conflict (although this status was not achieved until the end of the Afghan jihad). Abdullah 'Azzam
lauded Batterjee's group as being at the forefront of the jihad movement.[9]

Adil Batterjee played a significant role in the funding of al-Qa'ida,
as would be disclosed by Usama bin Ladin years later.[10] Batterjee's os-
tensible charity worked with the early incarnation of Bin Ladin's terror
organization, Maktab al-Khidmat to help outfit mujahidin during the Afghan campaign of the 1980s. But his trajectory for the mujahidin, like
'Azzam's, went far beyond that theater. His intentions were illustrated
in a 1991 book he published through BIF—under the pseudonym Basil
Muhammad—called *The Arab Volunteers in Afghanistan*.[11] By creating
portraits of the fighters who coalesced around that jihad effort, he hoped
to inspire other Muslims to join the caravan of fighters in emerging fronts
in the Islamic world. And clearly, his wealth went a long way toward making that vision a reality.

In the early 1990s Lajnat al-Birr al-Islami changed its name to Benevolence International Foundation in an apparent effort to expand its
reach and credibility. However, the two organizations remained under
Batterjee's control and driven by his assets. Through his endeavor, it truly
became an international organization with a wide reach. By the end of the
decade, it had set up offices in Azerbaijan; Bangladesh; Bosnia-Herzegov-
ina; Canada; China; Croatia; Georgia; the Gaza Strip; the Netherlands; in
Moscow and three republics in Russia's North Caucasus: Ingushetia, Dagestan, and Chechnya; Saudi Arabia; Sudan; Tajikistan; the United Kingdom;
in Illinois and New Jersey in the United States; and in Yemen.[12] But this
decade was not established solely through Batterjee's personal wealth; he
got the enterprise off the ground, but Muslim donors, believing they were
helping orphans and refugees, gave millions to BIF over the years.

One of the charity's officials, Suleman Ahmer, wrote in a 1999 email
that he feared BIF was misleading its donors—while the group claimed
that 100 percent of a special fund was going to serve orphans, he suggested the figure was in actuality nowhere near that amount.[13] Nonetheless, BIF continued to prosper as a premier Islamic charity, bringing in
$3.3 million in donations in 2000. In October of 1999 Enaam Arnaout
took a tour of Chechnya and Dagestan (Chechnya was then in the midst
of its second war with Russia, begun two months earlier after roughly

three years of ceasefire during which time foreign Salafists attempted to solidify their inroads into the Chechen conflict). Arnaout reported back to a BIF fundraiser on the roles that prominent Arab fighters were playing in the conflict.[14] In 1995 BIF sent camouflage uniforms, an X-ray machine, and $100,000 worth of antimine boots to the Chechen mujahidin (at the request of Suleman Ahmer, clearly demonstrating his knowledge of the support for militancy), along with smaller amounts of cash to support mujahidin activities against the Russian army.[15] Beyond the material needs of the fighters, Arnaout seemed to be enthralled by the narrative of the "Islamic movement" in Chechnya and Dagestan, moved—as were many other Arab jihad supporters—by the special place of Islam among the fighters and their morale and bravery. Arnaout made six trips to the region between 1995 and 2000, documenting the development of the mujahidin movement there.[16]

Meanwhile, in the United States, individuals tied more directly to al-Qa'ida central leadership (or at least tied to the organization that would solidify as al-Qa'ida in the late 1990s) were active on behalf of BIF. The foundation was incorporated in the United States, first in Palos Hills, Illinois, in 1992. Two years later, Mohammed Loay Bayazid, present at the founding of al-Qa'ida in 1988 and allegedly involved in attempts to procure uranium in Sudan in 1993–94, was pulled over by police in Northern California.[17] He was driving with Usama bin Ladin's brother, and his brother-in-law, Muhammad Jamal Khalifa. Bayazid presented the officer with an Illinois driver's license, which listed his address as the business office of BIF in Illinois, save for the suite number. The three were briefly arrested and then released. Bayazid (a naturalized American citizen) served, for a time, as president of the U.S. branch of BIF. He worked for BIF until he moved to Turkey in 1998.

But it was the raid on BIF's Sarajevo office in March 2002 that provided the definitive links to financing of al-Qa'ida militancy. Among the documents uncovered in that raid was a copy of the 1988 handwritten letter titled the "Golden Chain," listing twenty of the top financiers of Bin Ladin's mujahidin in Afghanistan, including Adil Batterjee.[18] Much more informative than the financial transactions or associations of its directors, the underlying mission of BIF demonstrates the role of financiers in the global jihad. The October 2002 indictment against Enaam Arnaout for racketeering and providing material support to al-Qa`ida included a study in which BIF concluded that where orphans were well taken care of, there was a corresponding improvement in the morale of soldiers.

These efforts to outfit mujahid soldiers on a battlefield were not the acts of the supporters of terrorism. Although the dramatically sinister acts of terrorists killing unarmed civilians have brought about a public recognition and popular momentum to confront such terrorist entities in legal, financial, and military capacities, seeing BIF and what it represents as simply support for terrorism is reductive to a dangerous degree. BIF, like the other purported charities that arose post–Soviet Afghanistan, is an embodiment of the Salafist calls for jihad that came in the decades—and even centuries—leading up to the attacks of 9/11. That jihad, reflective of its true meaning as an "effort" or "struggle," is not simply military. Contributions are required from all facets of the Muslim society in order for it to realize its full potential. The contributions of wealthy, devoted, and pious businessmen toward providing the Muslim soldiers with boots, tents, and blankets—and especially in vowing to care for their families should they die in battle—provided a social structure for the mujahidin that ensured they would not be left out in the cold.

In the early 2000s one of BIF's fundraisers paid visits to the Washington, DC area. Yusuf Wells regularly traveled to various communities in the United States raising money under a thin guise of charitable work for needy Muslims. According to BIF records submitted in the trial against Enaam Arnaout, Wells openly solicited donations in support of jihadi efforts abroad. Correspondences with donors show that at least some of those giving funds to BIF knew the destination of their donations—one states "may Allah continue to help the mujahideen." Some of Wells' public lectures were also in support of the Taliban.[19] In a letter to other BIF employees describing a May 2001 fundraising trip, Wells states as the reason for his lecture, "that the Taliban are not the bad guys that everybody says they are. And that they have done much good for the establishment of order in the country." Wells also met with the paintball group in Northern Virginia, who were convicted of providing material support for terrorist entities, among other charges. He discussed with those men the bravery of the mujahidin fighting in Bosnia and Chechnya, and watched jihadi videos with the group.[20] Wells represented the street-level activist working toward an international, long-term goal; he sought to play upon the believers' desire to support their brethren overseas through instilling, as 'Azzam did, the sense of a caravan of Muslim fighters across the globe.

As this enterprise grew in the 1990s, the vision of bolder ideologues like Qutb and 'Azzam, who saw a pan-Islamic nationalism rising across artificial, modern boundaries, came ever closer to reality. BIF and individuals like Batterjee and Arnaout were only two players among a much larger cast seeking to spread the jihadist spirit throughout the Muslim world. Bin Ladin and al-Qa'ida were only small elements of a much larger field of jihadists aiming to shape the world (in the longer or shorter term, depending on their strategic approach) around their conception of divine law and ideological purity. Following 9/11, the U.S. government designated dozens of charities operating in the country as supporters of terrorism, including a number associated with the Saudi government.

One form through which Saudi Arabia demonstrated its support for the mujahidin in Afghanistan was charitable, social, and educational outreach. In 1980 the Muslim World League (MWL), which receives Saudi government funding, hired Abdullah 'Azzam to head its education section from Peshawar. After 'Azzam, the office was run by Wa'il Julaydan, a wealthy Saudi financier who played a role similar to that of Adil Batterjee through different charities. One conduit through which Julaydan supported jihadist activities was the Rabita Trust, a financial arm of the MWL. The interconnectedness of these organizations is demonstrated by one of the titles Adil Batterjee holds on his curriculum vitae, Executive Director of the World Assembly of Muslim Youth (WAMY). WAMY was, for several decades, one of the largest international youth organizations serving the global Muslim community. It was also founded in 1972 in Riyadh as the youth wing of the MWL.

The Muslim World League was founded in Mecca in May 1962, a massive organizational structure with Muslim figures from twenty-two different Islamic nations. Funding and support for various Muslim causes around the world—while some constitute a support for terrorist activities—have been on the whole an effort to spread their version of Shari'a law into Muslim society. This effort took hold in the United States, but the organization—rather than being a direct sponsor of Islamist militancy—has been a superstructure for Salafi activism, often blurring the lines between acceptable Islamic activism and covert support for terrorist activities.

The MWL acted on the global stage much as the Muslim Student Association did in the United States. The analogous roles of the two organizations is not surprising—the MSA was founded by Ahmad Sakr, who was also a representative of the MWL to the UN. The MWL had an influence over Muslims that is much harder to quantify; although subtle, it laid the groundwork for Salafi precepts that affected mosques and Islamic organizations across the world. Thus, when advocating the necessity for action in any given situation, the MWL had previously instilled upon Muslim audiences its belief system and worldview. This long-term induction of Salafi thought into mainstream Muslim identity and belief may well be impossible to access in terms of its resulting violence, but in certain cases, as with BIF, al-Haramayn Foundation and other subsidiaries of the MWL, ostensibly charitable work was clearly done in the name of jihad.

The covert transfer of funds to support the mujahidin through charities served to beef up the enterprise of jihad in the 1990s to a great extent. But just as businessmen and financiers played their part, so too did highly skilled operatives who were able to engineer large-casualty attacks with limited resources. The man most commonly known as Harun Fazul provides a compelling example of Salafi ideology as the driver of radicalization and militancy, and also of an individual who advanced the movement's clandestine warfare—a weapon that was focused against American interests abroad as part of an al-Qa'ida strategy of targeting the West directly. But it would be a mistake to see him or any operative strictly within the confines of tactical operations; his example is noteworthy for its place in the evolution of jihadi tactics decades after the revolutionary calls of Sayyid Qutb or the strain of Salafi ideologues that preceded him. The example is also noteworthy for its place in the contemporary history of jihad, as someone of his abilities seems yet to have emerged organically in the West.

Abdullah Muhammad Fazul Husseine Mullah Ati,[21] alias Harun Fazul, was born into a small, middle-class family in Moroni, the capital city of Grande Comore, Comoros Islands.[22] His most likely true date of birth is August 25, 1972, although he has used multiple dates of birth on various alias documents in the course of his terrorist career. Fazul is fluent in Comorian, Swahili, French, and Arabic and, during his time as an al-Qa'ida operative, he has successfully disguised himself as Kenyan, Somali, Sudanese, Moroccan, Yemeni, and South Asian. Fazul is widely described as highly intelligent, well trained, and with connections to virtually every manner of criminal underground in Africa. He remains one the most dangerous international terrorists alive today.

Fazul was the youngest of six children. His parents separated during his infancy when his father chose to take a second wife.[23] Fazul's family was among the small middle-class of Moroni, with his sister and uncle both owning shops on one of Moroni's main streets. Fazul's family was also known on the islands as a devout one; his father was a well-known and esteemed imam. One of Fazul's early teachers recognized a propensity for violence within the young man. According to the teacher, Fazul would administer corporal punishments to fellow classmates for mistakes in their Qur'an recitation. After he cut the ear of one his classmates at age eleven, he was expelled from school.[24] While Fazul's early teenage years seemed to pass in an environment of moderate Islam and moderate political views, those who knew him described a definitive change when he entered into the madrasa of one of the Comoros' most prominent Salafi proponents.[25] The madrasa he entered, run by Soidiki M'Bapandza, a former Islamist opposition leader in the Comoros, stuck to a Saudi-designated curriculum. The madrasas under M'Bapandza also received funding from the al-Haramayn Foundation, a charitable arm of the MWL.[26]

After studying at the Saudi-funded madrasa, Harun received a scholarship to study overseas. He left the Comoros for Pakistan in 1990, just as the Soviet army was withdrawing from Afghanistan. During his first year in Pakistan he was recruited from his university studies to fight with the mujahidin, and moved to Bayt al-Ansar in Peshawar under Usama bin Ladin.[27] After passing through the screening given to recruits in their initial training, Fazul was invited by Bin Ladin's organization for advanced training, which consisted of two months' instruction in small arms, heavy weapons, explosives and bomb making, surveillance evasion, guerrilla warfare, and even "how to kill a president in full view while he's with his bodyguards."[28] His first mission was to help train Somali militants fighting the UN intervention in Somalia in the early 1990s,[29] where he claimed to have been directly involved in the 1993 Battle of Mogadishu. The following year, he began planning the U.S. embassy bombings while he was living in Kenya, and continued to work on the plan until its completion on August 7, 1998.[30]

Fazul was integrally involved in every step of the almost five years of planning that went into the embassy bombings. He was not yet in a leadership position within al-Qaʻida by that time, and was under the instruction of Wadih el-Hage, working under the cover of a fraudulent charity called "Help Africa People." The cell worked closely with Mercy International Relief Agency, an organization run by the Saudi Salafi ideologue Safar al-Hawali, as well as the Nairobi branch of the al-Haramayn Foundation, one of the charitable subsidiaries of the Mecca-based Muslim World League.[31] El-Hage served as a personal secretary to Bin Ladin, but also spent a significant amount of time in the United States. Born into a Catholic family in Lebanon in 1960, Wadih converted to Islam as a teenager while living in Kuwait where his father worked for an oil company, and was largely shunned by his family thereafter.[32] He sought religious instruction from a shaykh in Kuwait where he was first introduced to Salafi interpretations of Islam. In 1978 el-Hage moved to Lafayette, where he was accepted at the University of Southwestern Louisiana, pursuing studies in urban planning while he worked at a doughnut shop along with several other young Arab men.[33] Not long after beginning his college career, he left the United States for Pakistan to join in the burgeoning Afghan jihad against the Soviets. There, he became a follower of ʻAbdullah ʻAzzam, and stayed until 1985, when he returned to the United States to complete his college education. He graduated a year later, and moved to Arizona to start a family with a wife he met through a traditional arranged marriage. In Tucson el-Hage worked as a custodian for the parks and recreation department and held other minimum wage jobs; he gained his U.S. citizenship in 1989.[34] In December 1989 he met one of the leaders of the al-Kifah Refugee Center at an Islamic conference in Oklahoma City, and eventually became involved in the organization's fundraising and recruitment for jihad. El-Hage has connections to two murders in the United States and the 1993 World Trade Center bombings. In May 1996 the FBI raided el-Hage's home, seizing a computers and numerous documents, but due to a lack of Arabic translators, the material was left mostly neglected. He was convicted in May 2001 for conspiracy for his role in the embassy bombings, and is serving a life sentence in Florence, the supermax prison in Colorado, along with John Walker Lindh, Zacarias Moussaoui, Jose Padilla, and a number of other convicted terrorists.

Harun Fazul would eventually take over the leadership of al-Qa`ida's operations in East Africa, where he facilitated al-Qa`ida's entry into the blood diamond trade as a way to divert and launder al-Qa`ida money. After the embassy bombings, the United States began taking steps to freeze al-Qa`ida assets, and diamonds proved an ideal medium for protecting its monies. In the late 1990s he was a guest of Charles Taylor's Liberia.[35] Fazul led al-Qa`ida's East Africa cell in 2002–2007, planning a number of failed attacks, including the plot to take down Israeli airliners by shoulder-fired missile in Mombasa. During this time, he based his operations in a village on the island of Lamu off the Kenyan coast, where he acted as a preacher and instructor at a madrasa that he established—where he preached a clearly Salafi doctrine that put him at odds with local Muslims. A number of operatives joined him in Lamu planning the upcoming attack in Mombasa. Fazul was arrested for credit card fraud in July 2002 by Kenyan authorities, but escaped after his first day in custody.[36] Kenyan officials said they did not identify him as Harun Fazul. Following the unsuccessful plots, Fazul was reported to have taken a high-level position with the Islamic Courts Union around 2005.[37] Members of the elite U.S. anti-terrorism Task Force 88 are currently on the ground in East Africa searching for Fazul.

The story of Harun Fazul's trajectory from a radicalized youth in the Comoros to one of the most wanted (and difficult to capture) terrorist operatives in the world is remarkable. He emerged out of the post–Afghan generation of Salafi militants, compelled by the mujahidin's victory against the Soviets, but directed now against a Western enemy. The tactical environment for conflict had very clearly evolved, too; no longer was this a guerrilla war fought against an occupying army, but a covert battle fought primarily against soft targets.

The "de-territorialization" of Muslim populations, a concept introduced by the French scholar Olivier Roy, is another complicating component to the modern Salafi-jihadi problem.[38] Perhaps this trend began with the anti-Soviet campaign itself, as Arab Islamists abandoned conflicts in their home countries (such as Egypt), and joined into the larger pan-Islamist struggle against an outside enemy in Afghanistan. But the trend accelerated after that campaign drew to an end in 1989, as these fighters relocated and transitioned their jihadist efforts, scattered across many nations. The story of Wadih el-Hage is certainly one of territorial dislocation. He fought against Soviets in Afghanistan, with the support of the United States up until 1989 (while carrying out organizing efforts in Arizona, New York, and Texas), then fought the United States throughout the 1990s, from within the United States and from Sudan and Kenya. It is a fascinating example of covert conflict without loyalty to a physical home or nationality, but instead to a concept.

'Abdullah 'Azzam's preaching spread a message that, more than anything, said that Muslim pride could be restored and victory was possible, even when pitted against a military, political, and economic superpower. Thus, while the tactical environment changed, that basic message remained valid and relevant to a new generation. It resulted in a proliferation of Salafi-jihadi groups, a movement that seeks the purification of Islam and the concurrent military defeat of its enemies. The purification of Islamic doctrine has always been an essential component of Salafi reform, and while it seems overshadowed by militant operations conducted by jihadi activists, it is important to recall that that militancy is a by-product of the Salafi reform doctrine. The project of doctrinal purification—a much longer term enterprise—has been conducted in part by superstructure Islamic organizations such as the MWL, and it is hard to imagine their success being what it is without the tremendous oil wealth that backed their efforts.

Six

THE FLOW OF
SAUDI DOLLARS

"[T]he section of society that is instructed to make Jihad with its wealth is much larger than the section that is instructed to make Jihad with their lives."

—*Shaykh Yusuf al-'Uyayri[1]*

THE COVERT ORGANIZATIONAL efforts of militant Salafis formed the dominant trend in jihadi activism in the 1990s. While open battle-fields did exist—in Bosnia and Chechnya, for example—none would again be on the scale of Afghanistan in the 1980s. Much of that activism was undertaken by individuals who had no loyalty to an existing nation, but fought toward the ultimate creation of an Islamc state—a Caliphate—even if the prospects of its realization in their lifetimes was remote. This was true for leaders like 'Abdullah 'Azzam to operatives like Wadih el-Hage and Harun Fazul. But there was one state that, if not directly responsible at the top levels of its leadership, was at the least involved through the funding of some of its official charities—Saudi Arabia.

The question of Saudi complicity in terrorism is a tricky one, to put it mildly. There is no evidence to suggest that Saudi leadership has actively supported terrorist activity. In the 2000s, in fact, there was a fierce jihad-ist campaign against the House of Sa'ud, although the regime managed to put it down and forced many of its surviving leaders across the southern border into Yemen. The royal family of course also suffered an attempted coup of Mecca by Juhayman al-'Utaybi and his followers in 1979; that, like the more recent al-Qa'ida campaign, was carried out on the basis of regime corruption and a lack of the rulers' adherence to the "true" Shari'a. But the Saudi struggle with Salafi activists that most affected the country—and much more so, the Muslim world consuming the teachings of Saudi religious institutions—was the internal struggle with Muslim Brotherhood elements.

The Saudi regime kept close tabs on Brotherhood activities inside the kingdom, and the majority of its members kept their affiliation as quiet as possible. While the Brotherhood was allowed to exist within Saudi Arabia, its efforts toward activist organization were blunted. Within academia, however, clandestine Brotherhood members found a home and managed to thrive. The rapid expansion of the Saudi university system in the 1960s facilitated this role, and created a hub of Salafi activism for the decades to come that was, at least in part, independent from strict regime oversight. The creation of the Islamic University of Medina in 1961 and the King 'Abd al-'Aziz University in 1967 formed two enduring intellectual centers for Islamic thought. The Islamic University of Medina began with Abu'l-A'la Mawdudi as one of its trustees, and dozens of Brotherhood figures took up posts within the university, many from Egypt who were disaffected.[2] Mawdudi, the greatest contemporary to Qutb's brand of Salafism and the predominant figure of Islamism in South Asia, served on the Academic Council for the university until his death in 1979. The university has graduated a great number of influential Islamic leaders active in the United States, and many more alumni are active today in various branches of the Salafi movement.

The Islamic University of Medina was initially administered by the Saudi Grand Mufti Muhammad ibn Ibrahim Al al-Shaykh. The descendents of Muhammad ibn 'Abd al-Wahhab, known by the surname Al al-Shaykh (or family of the Shaykh), had traditionally held the authoritative role over clerical matters in the kingdom. But in the late 1960s and early 1970s their influence was waning, and there were growing tensions between that clerical family which inherited the legacy of Wahhabism, and the Muslim Brotherhood members taking on an increasingly powerful role within Saudi educational institutions. Ultimately the university was not a pawn of the Al al-Shaykh Salafis loyal to the regime, but dominated by Salafis instructed by the teachings of Qutb and Mawdudi, some of them members of the Brotherhood. The university had a tremendous impact on Islamic education worldwide: some 85 percent of its students were non-Saudi, hailing from Muslim countries the world over.[3] All this occurred at a time when the Saudi university system itself was growing exponentially—from 3,625 students in 1965 to more than 113,000 students by 1986.[4] It was a system richly endowed with the oil wealth of the state, where the vast majority of students' educations were dominated by Islamic studies.

As it first emerged on the scene, the Muslim Brotherhood was both an ally and a threat to Saudi Arabia, but the adept Saudi monarchy used it to its advantage. In its foreign policy, the Saudi state utilized the Brotherhood against secular regimes in Egypt, Syria, and Iraq, as well as in Afghanistan and Pakistan—where it forged an alliance with Mawdudi. Furthering that trend, the House of Sa'ud created two international bodies in the 1960s that were intended in part to redirect Muslim Brotherhood energies outside of the kingdom. The creation of the Muslim World League in 1962 and the establishment of the Organization of the Islamic Conference in 1969 were massive organizing efforts, driven in large part by the problem the Brotherhood posed internally. But this effort was also an attempt by King Faisal to establishment an Islamic bloc to compete with the Arab nationalism movement of Nasser's Egypt.[5]

In this climate, however, new strains of Salafi activism developed that would trouble the royal family in the decades to come. The *Sahwa Islamiyya* (Islamic Awakening) movement emerged as an outgrowth of the admixture of the Salafi-Wahhabi clerical establishment and the Muslim Brotherhood in Saudi Arabia in the 1960s; however, it remained closer to the Brotherhood in its outlook, and many view it as the Saudi version of that movement. Safar al-Hawali and Salman al-'Awda were leading members of the Sahwa Islamiyya, and two of its most influential practitioners. Safar al-Hawali received his PhD in Islamic theology from Umm al-Qura University in Mecca, where he was under the supervision of Muhammad Qutb, Sayyid's brother.[6] After multiple imprisonments, both have by now been reined in and effectively brought under state control, but their battle with the regime was emblematic of the Brotherhood struggle against the House of Sa'ud in the late twentieth century. They, along with other Sahwa leaders, adhered to the Brotherhood methodology of social and political organizing, with the tyranny and corruption of the royal family as the pivotal element of their platform.

In a well-known open letter, al-'Awda wrote in 1995, "Many of us talk among ourselves about the absence of social justice from our society. The problem lies in our failure to apply the rules of our religion (Shari`a), which was sent with a comprehensive reform message that included the spreading of justice, equality, and abolition of state and social oppression."[7] The Muslim Brotherhood struggle was clearly embodied in their work; the language is highly reminiscent of Sayyid Qutb. In it was a clear, emphatic call for implementing the Shari`a into social codes and law as the primary means of societal change.

The clerics of the Al al-Shaykh, and those loyal to it, fought a fierce rhetorical battle with al-'Awda and al-Hawali in order to discredit their ideology and the organizational efforts that stemmed from it. Three of the most prominent Saudi Salafi shaykhs—the Grand Mufti `Abd al-'Aziz ibn Baz, Nasir al-Din al-Albani (who was Albanian by birth) and Muhammad Ibn 'Uthaymin—issued public statements criticizing the actions of al-Hawali and al-'Awda on the basis of the Salafi *manhaj* (methodology), essentially excommunicating them as Salafis over their ties to the Muslim Brotherhood and statements about *takfir* (excommunication of fellow Muslims).[8] Al-Hawali and al-'Awda were more lenient in their defining of Muslim rulers as unbelievers, and in the spirit of Sayyid Qutb, using that as the basis for confronting their authority to govern. The two were imprisoned in 1994 for instigating uprisings in the Saudi city of Buraydah, and following that stint, were convinced by Saudi authorities, that they had no real chance of overthrowing the regime. They have since participated in "national dialogue" talks and led a number of Salafists with jihadi tendencies to turn themselves in to Saudi authorities.

When the Saudi monarchy began to realize that these breakaway Salafi ideologies threatened its survival, they mounted an informational campaign to shape Muslim belief, first at home, but ultimately, it became one of international consequence. The formal Saudi initiative to establish and defend a "pure" Salafi ideology began in earnest with the creation of the Permanent Committee for Islamic Research and Guidance (*al-lajna al-da'ima lil-buhuth al-'ilmiyya wa'l-ifta'*) by decree of King Faisal in

1971. It was a unified body of clerics—who have effectively overseen the doctrine of the Salafi movement within Saudi Arabia (their authority and legitimacy largely derived, in the eyes of Muslims, from their rule over Mecca and Medina)—set up to issue fatwas on belief, worship, and social issues. The Committee has been unflinchingly loyal to the royal family, guiding Muslims away from forms of activism that could threaten the House of Sa'ud's sovereignty.

'Abd al-'Aziz ibn Baz (more commonly known as Bin Baz) was perhaps the greatest beneficiary of the new Salafi establishment. He served as President of the Islamic University of Medina, one of the elite Salafi Islamic institutions, until 1971. Four years later, he was appointed to the ministerial rank of chair of the Permanent Committee, a position he held until 1993, when he became Grand Mufti of Saudi Arabia until his death in 1999.[9] Bin Baz studied under Muhammad ibn 'Abd al-Latif Al al-Shaykh and Muhammad ibn Ibrahim Al al-Shaykh, who was previously Grand Mufti of Saudi Arabia. With his insulated pedigree forged under the descendents of ibn 'Abd al-Wahhab, Bin Baz under the Saudi regime, he effectively institutionalized Salafism by creating a hierarchy of religious offices, officially within the Saudi government. Among those offices was that of the Muslim World League, where Bin Baz was a founding member and leading voice within the organization.[10]

Incidentally, Usama bin Ladin came to see Bin Baz as purely a puppet of the Saudi regime—and the Saudi government's involvement with Salafi scholars in the kingdom—as he described him in a 1996 interview with the now-defunct Australian-based *Nida' al-Islam*:

During the preceding two decades, the regime enlarged the role of Bin Baz (Grand Mufti) because of what it knows of his weakness and flexibility and the ease of influencing him with the various means which the interior ministry practices through providing him with false information. So, a generation of youth were raised believing that the most pious and knowledgeable of people is Bin Baz as a result of the media promotion through a well studied policy which had been progressed over twenty years.

After this, the government began to strike with the cane of Bin Baz, every corrective programme which the honest scholars put forward, further, it extracted a Fatwa to hand over Palestine to the Jews, and before this, to permit entry into the country of the two sacred mosques to the modern day crusaders under the rule of necessity, then it relied on a letter from him to the minister for internal affairs and placed the honest scholars in the gaols.[11] [Translation by the Australian staff of *Nida' al-Islam*]

■ ■ ■

The internal dynamics of competing Salafi currents in Saudi Arabia spread to the United States and around the world, where the flow of petrodollars invigorated Islamist activists. Between 1975 and 2002, the Saudi government spent over $70 billion on international aid, two-thirds of which went to building mosques or religious institutions.[12] Amid this outpouring, the Muslim World League and its subsidiaries' activities were generously supported. The MWL had grown to have some thirty branches worldwide by the mid-1990s, and a number of its offices supported the jihadi campaigns that flared up in the Balkans, the Caucasus, Afghanistan, and Tajikistan after the campaign against the Soviets concluded.[13] The competing Salafi trends in Saudi Arabia—the regime-loyal Wahhabite clerics, the Sahwa members, and the various post-Qutb activists—all seemed in support of the MWL; and for Saudis, it was a convenient way to divert activist attention outside of the kingdom.

These activities demonstrated the Saudis' support for the mujahidin abroad, an adept move by Saudi leadership to keep its Salafi population at bay, at least to an extent. Nonetheless, many such as Bin Ladin did come to see the Saudi-administered Salafi clerics who oversaw the MWL as a religious shield used to keep the regime in power. In that sense, the MWL was a balancing act for the Saudis that, for example, supplied arms to jihadi groups in Tajikistan and funded six militant training camps in Afghanistan in the 1990s, while under the auspices of the Saudi government.[14] As the Canadian branch leader of the International Islamic Relief Organization (IIRO), a MWL subsidiary, testified in a 1999 Canadian court case, "The Muslim World League, which is the mother of IIRO, is a fully government-funded organization. . . . In other words, I work for the government of Saudi Arabia."[15]

In the United States, the MWL and IIRO operated out of a shared office in the Washington, DC, suburb of Falls Church, Virginia, and was connected—by degrees—to a sprawling network of Islamic charities, think tanks, investment firms, and business fronts that were raided by federal agents on March 20, 2002. U.S. Treasury Department officials had previously deter-mined that another one of MWL's subsidiaries, Rabita Trust, had connec-tions to al-Qa'ida.[16] The Treasury Department designated the offices of the IIRO in the Philippines and Indonesia as supporters of terrorist organizations in August 2006 for their aid to al-Qa'ida-related insurgent groups (Jemaah Islamiya and the Abu Sayyaf Group).[17] Yet, the Saudi parent organization was not designated, despite officially sponsoring those offices.

An affidavit of Special Agent David Kane, who was investigating the case against the MWL and myriad other entities involved in the raids said, "Central to my investigation is the financial relationship between these entities [MWL and IIRO] and a New Jersey corporation, BMI, Inc."[18] BMI referred to Bait al-Mal, Inc. (The House of Wealth, in Arabic), an Islamic investing firm which was incorporated in March 1986. BMI was created by Soliman Bihieri, the only person to be convicted (for lying to federal agents) as a result of the massive investigation into terrorism financing involving a multitude of U.S.-based institutions. Prosecutors brought forward e-mails revealing that Bihieri was involved in financial dealings with Yaqub Mirza, a Pakistani engineer at the center of the case against a cluster of Saudi-backed Islamic charities and business entities in nearby Herndon, Virginia, known as the SAAR Foundation.[19]

On March 20, the same day agents raided the MWL and IIRO offices, more than a hundred other agents conducted raids against organizations tied to SAAR. The SAAR Foundation is named for Suleiman 'Abd al-'Aziz al-Rajhi, a Saudi billionaire who provided the organization with funding since its inception in the 1980s.[20] One of his relatives, Abdullah al-Rajhi, was a director at the Safa Group, one of the entities located along with SAAR at 555 Grove Street in Herndon. No arrests were made in any of the raids on March 20, which included sixteen locations in total. No businesses were closed either, but over 500 boxes of files and computer data were confiscated, filling seven trucks.

According to investigators, the individuals behind the SAAR enterprises operated over one hundred different organizations, over which they interchangeably served as officers, and many of which only existed on paper, with no physical premises. The majority of these fronts used the address of 555 Grove Street in Herndon.[21] These formed a complex network of shell corporations, investment banks, and charities that made it impossible for the investigators to determine precisely where all the money ended up. SAAR transferred $9 million to another Saudi charitable group in the Isle of Man, where banking secrecy laws make it difficult to trace.[22] SAAR's officers also have ties to companies under Youssef Nada, a Swiss businessman whose assets the United States froze for his involvement in terrorist financing. In all, the network had moved around, over the years, assets estimated at $1.7 billion, more than the total amount of assets frozen by the El Dorado task force that headed the investigation against them.[23]

Operation Green Quest was created within the Treasury Department in October 2001, as a multiagency enforcement effort aimed at "bringing the full scope of the government's financial expertise to bear against systems, individuals, and organizations that serve as sources of terrorist funding."[24] The operation maintained a dedicated field unit in New York alongside the expert financial investigators from the El Dorado task force made up of 185 employees from twenty-nine federal, state, and local agencies. Even with the nation's most successful financial crimes unit attached to the case, investigators were never able to bring terrorism charges forward; the money trail was too extensive.

At nearby 500 Grove Street, investigators raided another group tied to the SAAR Network, the International Institute for Islamic Thought (IIIT); the residences of Taha Jabir al-Alwani, Jamal Barzinji, Yaqub Mirza, and Ahmad Totonji were also raided on March 20, 2002.[25] Among those targeted in the investigation were the oldest-standing Islamist activists in the United States—two were among the original founders of the Muslim Student Association (the MSA being the first organization set up in America for activism in 1963). They hailed from the line of Muslim Brotherhood followers who brought the teachings of Hasan al-Banna and Sayyid Qutb to the West, intent on instilling that version of Islamic renewal into the community of American Muslims. In many ways this network remained close-knit in the United States; five of the network's senior executives lived on adjoining lots in modest two-story homes they built on twenty-two acres of land, named Safa Court, that an affiliate company bought and developed in 1987.[26]

The IIIT was created in Virginia in 1981, with a rather curious mission statement: "Towards Islamization of Knowledge and Reform of Islamic Thought."[27] It held a peculiar niche among Islamic organizations in the United States—it focused on promoting research and teaching that would advance Islamic concepts in various academic fields. What made it remarkable, however, was that it was merely one arm of this vast network, with its founders and officers intricately tied into the SAAR Foundation investigations. Ahmad Totonji and Jamal Barzinji, both founders of the IIIT in 1981, had been among the pioneers of Islamic activism with their founding of the Muslim Student Association in Illinois eighteen years earlier. MSA, once again, is the oldest and most widespread Islamic organization in the United States, and numerous sources have reported that its founders were members of the Muslim Brotherhood (Ikhwan al-Muslimun). The Brotherhood's internal documents plainly state that fact, found in this 1991 Guidance Council meeting: "In 1962, the Muslim Student Union was founded by a group of the first of the Ikhwan in North America, and the meetings of the Ikhwan became conferences and camps of the Student Union."[28] (The original Arabic document refers to the MSA founded by Totonji, Barzinji, and Ahmad Sakr as *Ittihad* or "Union," rather than "Association," but it is nonetheless referring to the same group.)

These early founders were part of the current of hybrid Salafi ideology that emerged out of Saudi Arabia (or through its educational institutions and/or their curriculum abroad) in the 1960s, though not all of them had close ties to Saudi Arabia. Barzinji and Totonji did not; both were born in Iraqi Kurdistan and received their education in the United Kingdom.[29] By the sixties, however, the Muslim Brotherhood movement was internationalized with the help of Saudi dollars, and its agenda was effectively being spread in Muslim institutions in western Europe and the United States. This group of early Muslim leaders were and are (they are still active in the Northern Virginia area) primarily concerned with organizational activism—spreading their beliefs to the young Islamic community in the United States through a network of dozens of Islamic organizations.

Jamal Barzinji lives across the street of Safa Court in Herndon from another pioneering activist from the sixties, Hisham Al-Talib, who was also an officer of the SAAR Foundation and Safa Group. Dr. Barzinji and his fellow activists had spent two and a half decades as fervent activists before developing that plot of land named for one of their enterprises, Safa Group; Safa is Arabic for "purity." After founding the MSA, Dr. Barzinji served as its president in 1972, was a year later a founding general manager of the North American Islamic Trust (NAIT), and maintains the title of vice president of IIIT since founding it in 1981, among his many positions and affiliations.[30]

Ahmad Totonji, like Barzinji, led a long career of activism, and was an officer of the SAAR Foundation, Safa Group, and their related entities.[31] He was also a leader within the World Assembly of Muslim Youth (WAMY) branch in Virginia. WAMY was created in Saudi Arabia in 1972, growing to 450 youth and student organizations and thirty-four offices worldwide.[32] Some of these WAMY offices have had ties to terrorism via jihadi conflicts in the Philippines, Kashmir, and other conflict zones that sprang up in the years following the end of the Afghan jihadi in 1989 and the dispersal of ʿAzzam's message that the jihad was just beginning, not ending.[33] While the MSA and its pursuant enterprises, NAIT and to some extent IIIT, were influenced by the Salafi strain embodied in the post–1960s Muslim Brotherhood, WAMY was of a different mold. Its funding came through Saudi pipelines like the MWL and IIRO, and the offices of all three organizations were involved in the Afghan jihad in the 1980s.[34] The WAMY office in Northern Virginia had been run by Abdullah Awad bin Ladin, a nephew of Usama's, who left immediately after the 9/11 attacks. The offices were raided in 2004, but no evidence of terrorist intent against the United States was brought forward against the organization. Dr. Totonji, according to his own website, held a key position in WAMY's operations in the United States during its formative years. He went on to serve as Assistant General of WAMY during the 1970s.[35] Ahmad Totonji's experience demonstrates some of the cross-pollination of Salafi currents that took place in the United States. These currents were connected to the Muslim Brotherhood presence in Saudi Arabia, those followers of Sayyid Qutb—many driven out of Egypt by Nasser, some connected through ideology—who gained so much influence in the kingdom's institutions of higher education.

Dr. Taha Jabir al-Alwani was born in Iraq in 1935 and received his PhD in Islamic Jurisprudence from al-Azhar University in 1973.[36] He had been in the al-Azhar system for his entire higher education, from the mid-fifties until completing his doctorate, during the execution of Sayyid Qutb and the purges of the Brotherhood. He found a home in Saudi educational circles, and was among the founding members of the Muslim World League. By 1975 he had arrived at the Imam Muhammad bin Sa'ud University in Riyadh, another premier Salafi institution in the Saudi system, and served as a professor there for ten years. In 1981 he helped found the IIIT and served as its president, and later also became an officer in the Safa Group, part of the SAAR network. Dr. al-Alwani came to be one of the leading figures in Islamic education in the United States, bringing his experience of the Salafi-dominated universities of Saudi Arabia, while at the same time working with Muslim Brotherhood activists like Barzinji and Totonji at IIIT.

Once settled in the United States, al-Alwani quickly rose to prominence as the president of the Fiqh Council of North America in 1988. The Fiqh Council "traces its origins back to the Religious Affairs Committee of the then Muslim Students Association of the United States and Canada in the early 1960s." It later became the Fiqh Committee of the Islamic Society of North America (ISNA) in 1980, before splitting off into its own entity in 1986.[37] The council primarily issued its fatwas through ISNA (and through them reached a great many Muslims in America). Dr. al-Alwani also went on to transform higher Islamic education in the United States. He founded the School of Islamic Social Sciences in Leesburg, Virginia (now the Cordoba University's Graduate School of Islamic and Social Sciences [GSISS]), where al-Alwani still serves as president.[38] In 2002 the GSISS was raided along with the SAAR entities. After opening in 1996, it was the first in the country approved by the Pentagon to train Muslim chaplains for the U.S. military; at the time of the raid, nine of the military's thirteen Muslim chaplains had studied there.[39]

Over the decades since 1962, a complex network of scholars, educators, and organizers have come to form a range of Salafi-inspired activists—some with official Saudi funds, some financed through wealthy Saudi citizens. These activists have had a tremendous impact on the American Muslim community: organizing it in the late 1960s, building institutions throughout the seventies and eighties (many of which, as noted in previous chapters, were supportive of the anti-Soviet jihad), and remaining active through influential associations like the Fiqh Council of North America in the nineties and after 9/11. U.S. courts have tried some of these organizations on terrorism-related offenses, such as that against the Holy Land Foundation. Put simply, the majority of these organizations did actively support jihad, though not against the United States, against Israel. Much of the financial support in the cases against Islamic organizations like those mentioned here went to support Palestinian groups, particularly Hamas after its birth in 1987. Jihad for Palestine has been a fashionable cause among virtually all the Salafi groups for decades, and between Saudi Arabian money and Muslim Brotherhood organizers, there were numerous voices in support of the Palestinians heard in America. The Palestinian conflict is a separate and complex one involving widespread Arab and Muslim interests, far beyond Salafism. The lines, however, among this plethora of Islamic groups and activists, have not always been clear, and some in the United States wanted the Saudis to pay for their part in fostering militant Islam leading up to 9/11.

On August 15, 2002, hundreds of families of 9/11 victims sued the Saudi government, including the members of its royal family, the MWL, IIRO, WAMY, SAAR, IIIT, al-Rajhi Bank, and numerous other charitable groups, investment banks, and the governments of Iraq and Sudan. It sued some of the long-time American Salafi activists such as Jamal Barzinji for their ties to the seventies- and eighties-era groups active in the Afghan jihad. They sought roughly 1 trillion dollars in damages, attempting to hold the Saudi regime and the efforts of Salafi activists they bankrolled responsible for sponsoring al-Qa`ida activities.[40] Seemingly countless legal motions by all the various parties involved dragged out over a number of years, and a federal appeals court ultimately rejected the suit. None of the facts regarding Saudi complicity—at any level—for the 9/11 attacks were heard before an American court. In August 2008 the U.S. Court of Appeals for the Second Circuit in Manhattan determined that they had no standing to hear the case unless the State Department had previously found a government to have provided material support for terrorism.[41] It was a highly ambitious lawsuit that did not, despite the length of all the facts provided, clearly demonstrate that the financial support that was widely flowing from the 1970s onward directly contributed to 9/11. The reality is, it did not. The attacks of September 11 were not the master plan of decades of Salafi activism stemming from the Saudi kingdom. Nor was it the culmination of the centuries of development of the Salafi movement, which of course began in the deserts not far from Riyadh with ibn 'Abd al-Wahhab in the late eighteenth century. Those attacks were simply one attack, in one campaign, of one particular militant outgrowth of the Salafi movement. It became increasingly more militant in its outlook following Qutb's martyrdom, and particularly with the Soviet jihad and ensuing campaigns fostered by 'Abdullah 'Azzam's movement; since then its violence has touch every inhabited continent. The origins of these manifestations of violence are too deeply rooted to be litigated.

There is no doubt that Saudi-funded efforts had an enormous impact on early Salafi activism in America. Through private citizens and the Saudi-backed MWL-type enterprises, significant Saudi funding was directed at the American Muslim community. The ideology that germinated in the United States as a result was, by the 1990s, clearly dominated by Salafi currents of thought. The influx of money and organizing skills laid the stage for the spread of Salafi belief among Americans, those beliefs being carried forward by multiple branches of the movement present in the West, from nonviolent activists to those confronting the United States with direct militancy.

Seven

SALAFI INFLUENCE
IN AMERICA

"Indeed the time is ripe for the Divine Sharī'ah"
—*Shaykh 'Umar 'Abd al-Rahman*[1]

BY THE 1990S one finds Salafism at its most diverse and fragmented in its more than two-hundred-year history. Much of this phenomenon has to do with the dispersal of the Muslim Brotherhood from, and within, Egypt in the 1950s and 60s. As a result of this process, pure ideological Salafi activists like 'Abdullah 'Azzam, fighting in defense of the global umma, formed movements independent from the Brotherhood activists that found a home in Saudi educational institutions from the sixties onward. But these efforts overlapped and mingled, as Saudi funding supported the mujahidin in Afghanistan and elsewhere in the nineties, and Brotherhood activists interacted with the adherents of Wahhabi thought in the kingdom's universities. What existed by the nineties was a movement made up of numerous distinct and largely autonomous groups, various branches descended from earlier Salafi thought competing among themselves for the representation of Muslim interests.

In America during the 1990s, this translated into a complex network of groups and personalities, with varying degrees of connectivity to Salafi thought and activism overseas. But significant questions of identity hang over the Muslim community in the United States. It is complex and diverse, true, but so many of the American Muslim organizations that have been active in the late twentieth century have roots with the founders of

Islamist activism in the United States, those that grew out of the Muslim Students Association in the early sixties and the subsequent endeavors of that pioneering circle of Salafi-inspired activists. It was a movement imbued with Brotherhood currents coinciding with the dispersal of its members from Egypt; those that were transplanted into Saudi Arabia and Iraq, namely. It was also connected to, in varying degrees, the Saudi financing that followed through a number of organizations operating in the United States, much of it through the complex network of businesses, investment firms, charities, and nonprofit organizations discussed earlier.

Clearly, the early activists of the 1960s had established a vast network, and over the decades it grew to include many shades of Muslim activists. Should groups like the Islamic Society of North America (ISNA)—the largest of the American Muslim organizations—be considered as Salafi, or Salafi-influenced? Certainly the organization had ties, through its leadership, to Salafism in Saudi Arabia. Muzammil Siddiqi, ISNA president from 1997–2001, earned his master's degree from the Islamic University in Medina, after which he held positions with the Muslim Students Association and the Muslim World League office at the United Nations in the 1970s.[2] Another one of ISNA's past presidents, Mohammed Nur Abdullah, received his higher education from Umm al-Qura University in Mecca in the late 1970s and early 1980s. Siraj Wahhaj, a prominent preacher and activist among American Muslims, was involved with ISNA since the eighties and was named as a vice president in 1997. He also studied at Umm al-Qura University in the late seventies. ISNA is now headed by Ingrid Mattson, a convert to Islam and Professor of Islamic Studies trained in the United States. It conducts a wide range of youth activities and holds large annual conferences that draw thousands of Muslims nationwide. Its activities have never suggested any militancy toward the United States, despite whatever connections its past leadership had to institutions of noted Salafi activism in Saudi Arabia.

The activism that sprouted out of the organizational work of Islamist groups in America beginning in the 1960s created an infrastructure that continued to grow for the next three decades. This infrastructure helped shape a new generation of Muslim activists in the United States and fostered them to be cognizant of the mujahidin's struggle with the Soviets in Afghanistan. The al-Kifah centers in Brooklyn and elsewhere in the

United States were evidence of this, along with large grassroots organizations like ISNA that supported their efforts. While the Muslim community itself in America is perhaps the most diverse in the world, composed of believers from virtually every country, activism inspired by Salafi thought (a great deal of it connected to Saudi institutions and individuals) has had a strong effect on the American Muslim community.

No official estimates are available on the Muslim population in the United States, and estimates have varied widely. The Council on American-Islamic Relations estimates there are between 6 and 7 million Muslims residing in America, while other groups say that number is closer to 2 million.[3] Ethnically, American Muslims are predominantly South Asian (33 percent), followed by African-American (25 percent) and Arab (25 percent); the remaining population comprises a wide range of ethnicities, including of course those converts of European ancestry.[4] Among this population, Salafi-oriented groups have found success by providing materials to American Muslims (like Qur'ans from Saudi Arabia, English language literature on Islam) who had been often isolated from the global Muslim community and establishing themselves as authorities on Islam in their communities by providing lecture series, fatwa services, free Arabic instruction, and meeting other needs. Although Arabs make up only about one-quarter of the American Muslim population, a clear majority of Muslim leaders in the United States are Arab. This trend may be related to the deference given to Arabic-speaking Muslims more broadly; the Qur'an is only considered valid in its original Arabic, and a great deal of importance is attached to mastery of the language. With the exception of a few South Asian activists, Salafism has been driven by Arabs and its ideological leadership is predominantly Arab. These demographic circumstances have made Salafi Islam readily accessible to American Muslims.

A number of self-designated "Salafi" institutions exist in the United States. One "Salafi Directory of North America" lists fifty-seven Salafi mosques in the country, spread out over twenty-one different states.[5] These, like the vast majority of contemporary institutions that identify themselves as Salafi, are affiliated with the official Salafi clergy in Saudi Arabia (those commonly referred to as Wahhabi). One such mosque is the *al-Masjid al-Awwal* (the First Mosque), which claims to be the first mosque in Pennsylvania, established in 1932. It offers a curriculum that includes teachings from Rabi' ibn Hadi al-Madkhali, a prominent Salafi shaykh from Saudi Arabia. Another example is Abu Mujahid Fareed Abdullah, one of the more prominent Salafi preachers in the United States; he is imam of Masjid al-Mu'min in Los Angeles and a graduate of Imam Muhammad bin Sa'ud University in Riyadh. These Salafi-identified mosques and institutions largely avoid political activism (eschewed by the clergy in Saudi Arabia), and focus their efforts on promoting the Salafi program for Islamic belief and worship among American Muslims.

This Salafi community in the United States is much less influential than that which grew out of the 1960s activism—the organizations descending from the MSA, like ISNA. It is, however, well connected by regular conferences and publications, as well as a number of Internet sites (such as salafitalk.net) that provide chat forums. These Salafi groups so closely affiliated with the official clergy in Saudi Arabia make extensive use of telelink to broadcast lectures to their followers in the United States These telelinks are typically lectures delivered from Saudi Arabia by phone-over-IP or webcam. Thus, a conference in California, Kansas City, or New York can provide a live lecture from the Grand Mufti of Saudi Arabia or the head of the Grand Mosque in Mecca. And Salafis have certainly used this technology to gain a wider American audience. Many of these telelink lectures—which are not broadcast to the public—have been organized by the Al-Quraan wa As-Sunnah Society of New York, which claims as its mandate: "Calling to Tawheed and Sunnah Upon the Manhaj of Salaf" (that is, calling Muslims to a message of God's Unity and the Way of the Prophet, along the methodology of the Salaf).[6] In addition, Salafi materials are distributed in the United States by sites like SalafiAudio. com, SalafiPublications.com, and troid.org (The Reign of Islamic Da'wah, based in Toronto). Online distribution of audio lectures and books has become the primary means of distributing Salafi materials in the United States.

On the educational front, Salafi currents from Saudi Arabia made their way into the United States through myriad nonprofit organizations—some of which have been described here—and schools funded directly by the Saudi government. The Institute of Islamic and Arabic Sciences in America (IIASA) was one of the most prominent of these schools operating in the states, and became a cause of concern for authorities when the school's curriculum came under scrutiny. IIASA was created in 1989 as one of six international affiliates of the Imam Muhammad Ibn Sa'ud Islamic University in Riyadh; other affiliates were established in Djibouti, Indonesia, Mauritania, Tokyo, and the UAE.[7] The school began formally offering a bachelor's degree in Islamic studies in 1992, equivalent to what one would receive from the Imam Muhammad bin Sa'ud Islamic University in Riyadh.[8] (It was not recognized in the Commonwealth of Virginia.) That institution was officially created in 1974, and like the universities of Umm al-Qura' University in Mecca and the Islamic University in Medina, it was a center for Salafis in the kingdom—both those of the Muslim Brotherhood and those aligned with the Saudi royal family. The curriculum of the university was dominated, by the late 1980s, by those Salafi elements aligned with the royal family, and it was that which was distributed through its international satellites.

IIASA was established in Fairfax, a northern Virginia suburb of Washington DC—where so much Salafi activism had been based over the decades. It received all of its funding through the Saudi Embassy, and its teachers were all technically employees of the embassy. In the edition of the website archived at the Library of Congress on November 14, 2001, the entire course curriculum—on the English website—was provided only in Arabic. It was an advanced course of Islamic studies similar to what a student would receive in Riyadh. The fall semester for 2001 offered Qur'anic studies and exegesis, hadith studies, Islamic doctrine I & II, "Modern Schools of Thought," research methodologies, the jurisprudence of worship, financial systems, Arabic grammar, and rather oddly, "Educational Psychology." Within this intense offering, the course on modern schools of thought stands out, as it—in keeping with the teachings of other Saudi Salafis—instructed students on the fallibility of recent Sunni schools of thought, emphasizing the necessity of returning to the Salaf (those first three generations of Muslims to succeed the Prophet) in formulating Islamic doctrine.

The course that clearly stands out from the others is "Educational Psychology"—it is not a subject of Islamic studies. In Arabic, the course is entitled "'ilm nafs tarbawi," 'ilm nafs meaning psychology, and tarbawi meaning pedagogical. Providing instruction on pedagogy, the study of being a teacher, implies that this course was at least partly designed to train a cadre of students to become educators themselves. The juxtaposition of this western, modern science—expounding upon how students best learn and develop, and in what setting—alongside the unbending and rigid austere Islamic coursework is remarkable. Salafism, which began in such adamant opposition to change—initially against changes in Islamic practice that ibn 'Abd al-Wahhab deemed agents of corruption and heresy—came to accept modern ways of the world. Ideologically, it is by its nature unchanging; innovations in religious belief are a sin, nothing after the three generations of Salaf is valid as a basis for law. Yet, technological advancement and scientific endeavors were accepted and lauded. Salafis certainly embraced modern methods of distributing information, as well as modern educational methods, both of which were well utilized in the pursuit of spreading their worldview.

The program was an ambitious one in the United States. It boasted,

"The Islamic Studies Department is the only one of its kind in America, offering a complete undergraduate program in Islamic studies. Faculty members who are specialized in their respective fields teach the program in Arabic. The curriculum is equivalent to those of universities in Muslim countries."[9]

IIASA's Islamic studies program even achieved its goal to "foster academic cooperation with departments of similar orientation at American universities," stating on its website, "[a] prime example of this is the academic cooperation with the Harvard University School of Law, which won a large grant from the Embassy of Saudi Arabia to enable it to establish a department of Islamic law." But the university was hardly of a similar educational philosophy as that of Ivy League universities. Applicants needed a high school diploma, the "mastery" of speaking and writing Arabic, and demonstration of the memorization of one-thirtieth of the Qur'an. These prerequisites ensured that only dedicated Muslims would be accepted, clearly weighted toward native Arabic speakers. During summer and extended breaks in classes, students could participate in extramural conference and community events in the Washington metro area. The program also offered imams to mosques in the area, and even to mosques and Islamic centers "in the continent [sic]" during the holy month of Ramadan.

On the occasion of the (Saudi-designated) one hundredth anniversary of the Kingdom of Saudi Arabia in 1999, IIASA hosted a symposium entitled, "The Role of the Kingdom of Saudi Arabia in Calling for Islamic Solidarity and the Establishment of Islamic Organizations." The Saudis were pleased to present the American Muslim and academic communities with the efforts it had made in supporting the global Islamic community (*umma*) through its activism and generosity. A talk by Abdullah Nasseef lauded the Saudi role in activism: "Praise is due to Allah SWT and then to the kings of Saudi Arabia who supported this pioneering organization and other non-governmental bodies such as the Muslim World League in Makkah in 1962 and the World Assembly of Muslim Youth in Riyadh in 1973."[10]

Dr. Nasseef had good reason to be thankful. He had served as the secretary general of the Muslim World League, and was then vice chairman of the World Assembly of Muslim Youth. He also served on the advisory council (*majlis al-shura*) to the Saudi royal family. His presence at the symposium—and its unambiguous title—exemplified the role IIASA played in the Muslim educational community in America. Things would change dramatically for this bold educational endeavor, however, roughly twelve years after the program launched.

In January 2004 the U.S. State Department revoked the diplomatic visas of sixteen IIASA employees. State Department officials characterized the move as "an ongoing effort to protect the homeland."[11] Eleven of the sixteen employees whose visas were revoked were Saudis. One of them, Ibrahim ibn al-Kulaib, was an active organizer for Saudi Salafism in the area. He also founded the Islamic Foundation of America, based in Springfield, Virginia, which ran a mosque and had extensive prison outreach funded by the Ministry of Religious Affairs in Saudi Arabia. This move came after diplomatic talks that resulted in a decision from Riyadh to cease sponsorship over IIASA. In July federal agents raided IIASA, seizing documents and computers, but made no terrorism-related arrests of anyone working at the institute then or in subsequent investigations. The raids in July were by then deemed a joint U.S.-Saudi effort to crackdown on ideologies that engendered intolerance and violence.[12] Through the diplomatic arrangements that were made months earlier, Saudi was again spared any culpability in spreading such ideologies.

The raid may have been brought about not solely by the ideology taught at the institute, but by its proximity to the activities of a group of young Muslim men arrested and tried for preparing to join the jihad in Pakistan and Afghanistan—the so-called Virginia Jihad Group. IIASA had served as an informal meeting place for the group and place of worship.[13] The eleven men in that group were arrested in the summer of 2003. They had used paintball games hosted at a property in rural Virginia, not far from Marine Base Quantico and the FBI Academy, to train for jihad. There was speculation that Jaafar Idris, one of the sixteen IIASA employees whose visa was revoked and who was also a mentor to the convicted spiritual leader of the group, was the target of the raid.[14] Jaafar Idris was also president of the American Open University in Alexandria, Virginia, and he had helped found the Islamic Foundation of America in nearby Springfield with Ibrahim ibn al-Kulaib.[15] But Jaafar Idris, a Sudanese national with Saudi citizenship, had never shown any signs of supporting militant jihadi activities against the United States. The case of IIASA would prove once again how difficult it was to prosecute ideology that fosters violence for federal agencies.

The Saudi higher education program at IIASA was not a singular effort at Islamic education in America. They also supported a K-12 Islamic school with two campuses in northern Virginia. That school, the Islamic Saudi Academy, was founded in 1984, and grew to about 1,300 students between the Alexandria and Fairfax campuses.[16] Its curriculum was in both English and Arabic, but roughly 30 percent of the student body was made up of Saudi citizens.[17] The school referred to its curriculum as "dual American and Middle Eastern," but much of the content was derived from Saudi textbooks and some of the syllabi for the Arabic portion of the classes were taken directly from Saudi schools. The school also receives the majority of its funding from Saudi Arabia, and the Saudi Ambassador to the United States was the chair of the school's board of directors (he is currently the honorary chair).[18] By 2007 this caused significant concern among some U.S. lawmakers, and hearings by the U.S. Commission on International Religious Freedom urged that the school be shut down.

■   ■   ■

In late August 2001 the Saudi minister responsible for the two holy mosques (those in Mecca and Medina, the holiest in Islam) arrived in Washington for a series of meetings with the network of Islamic organizations his government had helped fund or create in the United States. Many were conveniently in the Washington, DC, area; they included the Islamic Foundation of America founded by Ibn al-Kulaib and Idris, the Muslim World League office, and other Islamic charities and nonprofits in the United States.[19] That minister, Salih al-Hussayen, was at one time a director of the SAAR Foundation, the organization at the center of the financing probe that would get under way in the months after 9/11. During his travels in the Washington, DC, area, he stayed at a Marriott Residence Inn in Herndon, Virginia, only a half-mile away from the SAAR Foundation offices and the cluster of groups associated with them.[20]

Three of the 9/11 hijackers who would fly Flight 77 into the Pentagon the following day, Hani Hanjour, Khalid al-Mihdhar, and Nawaf al-Hazmi, were staying at that same hotel with Salih al-Hussayen on the night of September 10, 2001.[21] There is no evidence that Hussayen met with any of them, however. According to an FBI agent who attempted to interview Hussayen and his wife about their proximity to the hijackers and whether the parties met, Hussayen feigned a seizure and was taken to the hospital.[22] Doctors there found nothing wrong with him. But agents were not able to interview him again and he and his wife left on September 19, when air travel resumed. Hussayen's stay at the Marriott Residence Inn alongside the hijackers may have been coincidence. Northern Virginia was a hub of Islamist activity, especially in the 1990s, with pockets of well-developed activist networks dotting the landscape. It is strange for a Saudi official to stay in rather inauspicious lodging such as that, and there seems no other reason than to be near the numerous Islamic organizations operating there with whom he had meetings. In that community, the 9/11 hijackers, trainees for jihad in the paintball group, imams like Jaafar Idris, Saudi officials, and activists of many persuasions crossed paths or had interactions with the same institutions.

During his trip to America, Hussayen also paid visits to New York and the Midwest. One of the organizations he met with was one he had donated to, where his nephew also worked as a website administrator. That group, the Islamic Assembly of North America (IANA), was based just outside Ann Arbor, Michigan, in a single-story, modest building in Yp-silanti. It was created in 1993 with a focus on missionary (da'wa) work. According to its website, IANA distributed 530 packages of literature to prison inmates, which included a series of audiotapes on Islam, a Qur'an, and several books on Islamic thought.[23] The titles were not made available. IANA sponsored regular seminars, workshops, and lecture series, many of them held at the Islamic Center of Ann Arbor—the same mosque used by students at the University of Michigan and its Muslim Student Association—where it found a large audience of both American converts and Muslims of diverse heritage.

IANA was an enthusiastic proponent for Islamic activism, Salafism in particular. The organization ran on a somewhat meager budget compared to the amounts of money financing some of the groups in northern Virginia. The group had an operating budget of around $500,000 annually. A former chairman of IANA, Muhammad al-Ahmari, told the *New York Times* that, as of 2001, roughly half of his organization's funding came from the Saudi government, with the remainder coming primarily from private individual donations from the Gulf. One of those individuals was Salih al-Hussayen, who gave $100,000 to IANA.[24] The group had its roots in earlier Islamist organizing. IANA grew in part out of Dar Makkah, a defunct organization started in Denver. Dar Makkah's former director, Mohammed Al-Ahmari, became IANA's director, first incorporating in Colorado.[25] Shortly after its incorporation, IANA purchased the property in Ypsilanti and relocated its operations.

IANA alludes to its Salafi activism agenda on its website, "[I]f we desire to achieve the final goal of reviving the Islamic nation to its proper state and condition, then we, while working for Islam, must return to its original spirit of work and action."[26] In its mission statement, it also declares that the Shari'a calls for them to engage in a "comprehensive form of Islamic work . . . based on the principles of Ahl al-Sunnah wa al-Jama'ah [the people of the Prophet's tradition and the group, i.e., the mainstream of Sunni adherents] and the guidance of the pious forefathers."[27] The pious forefathers, of course, referred to the Salafi, those first three generations of Muslims in Islamic history. This comprehensive work aimed to coordinate the da'wa work of numerous Islamic groups, to guide them upon their ideology—"the proper Islamic methodology." Among IANA's other goals was to "[t]ie the Muslims of America into what is happening in the Muslim world and assist them in understanding the events and the implications of the current events" and "[a]ssist the oppressed and tyrannized scholars, Islamic workers and Muslim masses in any locality." No other Salafi organization operating in the United States had been so bold in its activist objectives. In achieving this, the founders determined:

> IANA will use a number of sound means and methods, including: conventions, general meetings, da'wa-oriented institutions and academies, books of an academic, da'wa-oriented or Islamic thought nature in both Arabic and English, magazines and other periodical literature, technical programs, youth programs, investment projects, and other means possible in this country.[28]

Indeed, IANA carried out robust publishing work. It published magazines like *Assirat al-Mustaqim* ("the Straight Path") and *Al Asr* ("the Era") that covered militant Islamist movements such as those in Algeria, the Balkans, and Chechnya in the 1990s.[29] An issue published on Al Asr's website in May 2001 contained three fatwas endorsing terrorism. One of these came from Salman al-'Awda, stating that "martyrdom" operations were permissible under the conditions that a suicide attack would "gain supremacy for the word of God" or "harm the enemy, through the killing and the wounding . . . or demoralize the enemy when they see that only one Muslim could do such damage." Another fatwa from Kuwaiti Salafi cleric Hamid al-'Ali clarified the difference between different types of suicide bombing operations, lauding the utility of destroying a "vital enemy command post." The fatwa even suggested a modern-day warfare method: "to crash one's plane on a crucial enemy target to cause great casualties."[30]

The administrator for this online jihadi publishing endeavor was Salih Hussayen's nephew, Sami Omar al-Hussayen, who, in the early 2000s, was then a graduate student in Idaho. He was tried on charges of supporting terrorism through his administration of IANA's websites; ultimately he was not convicted of those but on visa fraud charges, for failing to disclose his work for IANA on immigration forms. Al-Hussayen maintained—until 2003, when he was tried—over a dozen networked web-

sites, including the popular www.islamway.com, as well as www.iananet.
org and www.ianaradionet.com, www.alsunnah.com, www.alasr.ws, and
registered www.alhawali.org for Saudi cleric Safar al-Hawali. Islamway.
com hosted videos of combat scenes from jihad in Bosnia and others of
al-Qaʿida members engaged in battle. Another one of that network's websites, www.al-multaqa.com, published pieces such as "Jihad in the Qur'an
and the Sunnah," "The Objectives and Aims of Jihad," and "The Religious
and Moral Doctrine on Jihad."[31] Another one of IANA's websites, www.az-
zam.com, named of course for ʿAbdullah ʿAzzam, was shut down by the
FBI in 2002.

IANA also fulfilled its mission of hosting Islamic conferences. While
many were held locally in the Ann Arbor area, they also held national conferences annually, typically in the Midwest. According to the Investigative Project, a research group that does exposés on terrorism in
America, al-Qaʿida recruiter ʿAbd al-Rahman Dossari spoke at three IANA
conferences in the early 1990s.[32] IANA also had ties to the Virginia Jihad
group's leader Ali al-Timimi. Al-Khafagi, an Egyptian national, pled guilty
to bank fraud in Detroit in 2002 and was eventually deported back to
Egypt. Al-Timimi and IANA President Bassem Khafagi attended a conference together in Beijing in 1995. IANA also had provided funding to Jaafar
Idris' American Open University in Fairfax, Virginia.[33]

Umar Lee, who describes himself as a "former member of the Salafi
movement," maintains an active blog about Muslim affairs, and docu-
mented his observations on the Salafi community in the United States.
Lee writes that "[b]y the time the 1990s rolled around, Salafis were becoming a major force in the area" due to the presence of IIASA, the MWL, and
WAMY, the "emergence of a vibrant African-American Salafi community,"
and "two men who would become famous the world-over to Salafis": Jaafar Idris and Ali al-Timimi, as well as the American Open University that
promoted their line of teaching and approach to Islam.[34] Al-Timimi and
Idris ran a very small office in the District of Columbia, initially calling
their organization the "Society for the Adherence to the Sunnah," which
eventually came to be Dar al-Arqam, housed at the same office building
on 360 S. Washington Street in Falls Church, Virginia, as the Muslim
World League and the International Islamic Relief Organization.

Lee described the annual IANA conferences as an integral part of spreading Salafi da'wa, and that to find acceptance in the IANA circle, one did not have to label oneself a Salafi, and "loyalty to the Saudi throne" was not required.[35] This made IANA more accessible to a wider Muslim audience in America, and helped it gain popularity, especially among young Muslims and converts. According to Lee, "The salafi books and tapes were flowing like a river," and it was not uncommon to find some of the brothers with hundreds of tapes in their collections, competing to get the latest. IANA was a big part of spreading this movement, as was the Salafi community in the Washington, DC, area. When IANA virtually dissolved after the intense post-9/11 scrutiny it received, its officers, members, and followers were dispersed into other movements, and some simply fell off the scene. Lee says some exchanged their long flowing beards and Islamic garb for neatly trimmed beards and suits and ties. Some moved to other communities like Houston, Texas, where the Al-Maghrib Institute is headquartered. It offers Islamic studies coursework through weekend seminars and extensive online offerings, as well as hosting a popular discussion board. There has also long been a thriving activism scene, with many connections to the Brotherhood, in the Richardson area outside Dallas, over which Al-Maghrib competed for membership and recruitment.

Through the activities of Minister Hussayen and his nephew, IIASA, and the flow of student-activists from Salafi universities in Saudi Arabia, Saudi involvement seems to abound in Salafi activism in the United States. But for the most part, it has always been a step removed from acts of terrorism. The Salafism practiced in Saudi Arabia and exported around the world did, however, share much the same ideological basis and doctrine, and it was not a far leap for some Salafi activists to adopt a view of jihad as obligatory in certain circumstances. Clearly, IANA and its affiliate websites glorified the jihadi movement in Muslim conflict zones, and were moving toward advocating militancy openly through publishing the fatwas of Salafi-jihadi clerics like Hamid al-'Ali. The IANA experience—and the case of Ali al-Timimi in particular—demonstrated very clearly how one could traverse the ideological spectrum of Salafism from educational and missionary work to participating in militant jihad, all within the framework of activism in the United States.

Eight

ANATOMY OF A TERRORISM CASE

"In those days, young men were very interested in jihad and martyrdom."

—*Ali al-Timimi*[1]

SALAFISM CAN BE a rather amorphous subject, an ideological movement with branches, divisions, and nuances. It has been the driver of violent acts and militant groups, but much more broadly the driver of numerous forms of activism toward instituting a particular interpretation of Islamic law onto Muslim societies worldwide. In order to highlight the importance of this ideology and how it has influenced Muslims to join militant causes, it is necessary to look at the specifics of a terrorism case. The group led by Ali al-Timimi, the imam and scholar who came to be a well-known thinker in Salafi circles, provides a clear example of how young men can be influenced by this movement and convinced of the necessity of violent action as a remedy to the ills of the Muslim nation. In addition, the group's diversity is representative of the global nature of the Salafi message—they comprised both born Muslims and converts; white, black, East and South Asian.

In the summer of 2003, eleven men were arrested and charged with conspiring to wage war against an ally of the United States, India, among other charges related to their intent to become mujahidin. The group, known in the media as the "Virginia Jihad Network," was best known to the public for their paintball games, in which they simulated combat

91

scenarios as part of their training for jihad. The eleven men were charged with forty-two counts in a seven-part conspiracy, including knowingly enlisting in armed hostility toward the United States, and the intentional participation in military activities against a foreign state with which the United States is at peace. The conspiracy also described members of the groups' related illegal acquisition and transport of firearms and use of false or altered passports.[2]

In the fall of 2002 the FBI's Washington DC field office received two similar tips from local Muslims: Ali al-Timimi was running "an Islamic group known as the Dar al-Arqam" that had "conducted military-style training," according to agents.[3] In February 2003 the FBI raided al-Timimi's home in Fairfax, Virginia, and discovered numerous Islamist and some jihadi texts. In May, federal agents carried out raids on the group members' six homes as part of the investigation, including those of Muhammed Aatique, in Norristown, Pennsylvania, and Masoud Khan, in Gaithersburg, Maryland. At Khan's house in Gaithersburg, they collected an AK-47-style rifle, another rifle, a shotgun, and a .45-caliber pistol, and in a baby's room, a document entitled "The Terrorist's Handbook," which contained instructions on how to manufacture and use explosives and chemical weapons. Also uncovered were photographs of the Washington Monument, the National Atomic Museum, and the FBI building. In those raids, agents executing a search warrant also seized a document from Idris Surratt listing "plans for actions if something kicks off," describing the need for group members to join the NRA, presumably as a cover for their firearms training.[4] In a search of Ali Asad Chandia's home and car, agents discovered audiotapes praising bin Laden and a CD showing the hijacked planes smashing into the World Trade Center and voices chanting "Allahu Akbar" in the background.

On June 27, 2003, the indictment against the group was unsealed, and FBI agents executed arrest and search warrants for members and their homes in Pennsylvania, Virginia, and Maryland, arresting six of the eleven defendants. Two were already being held on other charges. At the same time, agents had been cooperating with Saudi Arabian security officials, and eventually executed arrest warrants for two of the members who had been in the kingdom, Mahmoud Hasan and Sabri Benkhala. Federal prosecutors maintained that the group sought jihad training from Lashkar-e-

Taiba (LeT—an al-Qaʿida affiliate based in Pakistan), in order to support the Taliban regime as U.S. forces invaded Afghanistan in late 2001.

Five days after the attacks of September 11, Yong Ki Kwon, one of the group members and a naturalized American Citizen from South Korea, organized a dinner at his home with their spiritual mentor, Ali al-Timimi. At the meeting, which came to be a key event in the FBI's investigation, al-Timimi told a select group of his followers (during which he urged secrecy), that the young men were obligated to support the Taliban, Mullah Omar, and "the Arabs with them" by "body, wealth and word even if some find that distasteful."[5] At the dinner hosted by Kwon shortly after September 11, al-Timimi also told the young men that American troops would be legitimate military targets if they arrived in Afghanistan to topple the Taliban, and—as ultimately proven by the prosecution—encouraged the young men to receive military training from LeT. Al-Timimi was sentenced in 2005 to life imprisonment for inciting his followers to jihad.

As Kwon and others testified, this meeting set the stage for al-Timimi to clandestinely encourage his followers to wage or support violent jihad on behalf of their Muslim brothers, even if that meant taking up arms against the United States. Yet, the training the young men received was, in actuality, not very substantial. Further, the vast majority of the group's firearms training in the United States was conducted legally and no specific plans were uncovered to carry out an attack inside the United States or to specifically target Americans. None of the group's members would actually fight in Afghanistan nor would the FBI find evidence to prove that the group had specifically plotted to conduct acts of terrorism, but it did prove the group's members intended to fight against American forces in Afghanistan. Ten of the eleven were sentenced to terms ranging from forty-six months to sixty-five years in prison, one (Sabri Benkhala) was acquitted, but later charged and convicted for perjury related to his testimony in the case.

COMING TOGETHER AROUND COMMON BELIEFS

Members of the group met at various times in the late 1990s through the Muslim community in the Washington, DC, area. By early 2000, members of the groups were drawn toward Salafi Islam, as espoused by al-Timimi and others in his circle, and engaged in discussions on matters of religion,

including jihad.[6] That community—adhering to a similar set of Salafi beliefs—included the Dar al-Huda Islamic Center in College Park, Maryland,
the Islamic Assembly of North America (IANA), and a set of Saudi Salafi
shaykhs, among others. But the group's focal point was the Dar al-Arqam,
also known as the Center for Islamic Information and Education, located in the same office complex as the prominent Saudi-based groups, the
Muslim World League and International Islamic Relief Organization, at
360 S. Washington St. in Falls Church, Virginia. The center was founded
by al-Timimi and others in 1999, in order to provide English language
instruction on Islam to Western Muslims.[7] It became apparent, however,
that the center had other educational objectives in mind.

Ali Mehdi al-Timimi was born in the United States in 1963 to parents
who immigrated to Washington, DC, from Baghdad.[8] He attended American schools, including the prestigious Georgetown Day School in Washington, until his parents moved to Saudi Arabia in 1978. At age fifteen, in
1987, al-Timimi began Arabic language training at Manaret High School
in Riyadh, where he rapidly progressed in spoken and written Arabic. He
was also instructed in Islamic worship and practice as interpreted by the
austere Salafi tradition in Saudi Arabia. Al-Timimi continued his studies
there, and undertook his earliest ideological training in his second year
with one of today's best-known English-speaking Salafi Imams, Bilal Phillips.[9] The Canadian-born Phillips was a graduate of the Islamic University
of Medina, one of the most influential institutions for Salafi learning. Al-
Timimi was influenced by Phillips, who emphasized the importance of
strict adherence to the Qur'an and Sunna (teachings of the Prophet), as
he had learned in his own university instruction.[10] Ali returned to Washington in 1981 to begin college, with a newfound devotion and commitment to the Islam he had experienced in Riyadh.

Attending George Washington University, al-Timimi found that aware-
ness and perceptions of Islam among Americans had changed greatly
since 1978 when he left the United States. The Iranian revolution and
Juhayman al-'Utaybi's takeover of the Great Mosque in Mecca in 1979
had brought Islam into the political discussions of Americans to a much
greater extent than at any time in his life. His interest in, and his devotion to, Islam continued throughout his college years, and he opted to
return to Saudi Arabia in 1987 to attend Phillips' alma mater, the Islamic
University of Medina. Al-Timimi returned to the Washington area a year

later to pursue a career, at his family's urging. He had, however, formed close bonds with the Saudi clerical establishment that provides instruction at the university, including the now former grand mufti of the kingdom, 'Abd al-'Aziz bin Baz. Despite his early attachment to Saudi clerics, he was open to rational methods (Bin Baz famously insisted the world was flat in a 1976 fatwa) and continued his pursuit of science, eventually defending his PhD dissertation at George Mason University in Virginia in computational biology.[11] In one of his lectures, he surprised his audience by claiming that contemporary Salafi thinkers, on account of their doctrinal rigidity, ran the risk of turning themselves into a "country club" of believers.[12]

Throughout the 1990s, al-Timimi delivered lectures at Islamic conferences and grew a small but growing audience, although most topics covered were doctrinal and apolitical. According to Umar Lee, the "former Salafi,"

> Sheikh Ali became such a popular local figure that his classes became "the place to be" for the youth of the masjids [mosques] throughout the D.C. area. People would come who were raised in Muslim homes. Some were even secular or sufi and generally very far from the Salafi Da'wa.
>
> The attraction of Sheikh Ali was the fact that this was a man who was born and raised in America, spoke in clear English, and not only had a great knowledge of the *din* (religion) but was college educated, an IT professional, a cancer researcher, and a very serious intellectual. This was a man who could take the knowledge of the Salaf and make it applicable to your everyday life and could speak in a language we all understood. . . . How he differed from the other Salafi leaders in the community is that he would—from time to time—address political issues and acknowledged the world that we live in.[13]

■   ■   ■

Hammad Abdur-Raheem met fellow group members Caliph Basha and Donald Surratt (later Idris Surratt) at Prince George's Community College of Maryland in 1996. In 1998 Abdur-Raheem transferred to Northern Virginia Community College and moved the short distance to

Northern Virginia, where another member of the group, Ibrahim al-Hamdi, had also studied.[14] Abdur-Raheem was born Allen Walter Lyon on September 6, 1968. Born and raised in the Maryland suburbs of Washington, he joined the army after graduating from high school. According to court documents, Abdur-Raheem was raised Christian but became increasingly interested in Islam. He converted to Islam in 1994 during the course of his military service (following a tour of duty in the first Gulf War).[15] He was honorably discharged in 1996, after which he moved back to Maryland to attend Prince George's Community College. In the late 1990s he became concerned over the conflict in Chechnya, and sought ways to support Muslims fighting Russian forces there. Abdur-Raheem created an organization, "Chechan Zakat (sic)," to collect funds purportedly for Chechen refugees which he admitted was, in reality, designed to deliver funds to Chechen mujahidin.[16]

Yong Ki Kwon was a central figure in the group. According to his court testimony, he met al-Timimi and other group members at an IANA conference in Chicago in 1997—the same year he converted to Islam. He attended college at Virginia Tech with fellow group member Muhammad Aatique and Masoud Khan's brother in the late 1990s. Kwon stayed with the Khan family, living in their basement after graduating from Virginia Tech. Masoud Khan was born in Washington, DC, in 1970, but returned to his father's native Pakistan at the age of four, and spent part of his childhood years in Saudi Arabia.[17] At age seventeen, Khan moved to Gaithersburg, Maryland, where he briefly attended the Gaithersburg High School before completing his GED. Khan took online courses through the American Open University, the distance-learning school founded by Jaafar Idris in late 1995. After completing an exam through the university, Khan earned a scholarship to study at the Riyadh University of Saudi Arabia.[18] Graduating from Riyadh University after three and a half years, he returned to the Washington, DC, area in early 2000 and sought a marriage, arranged by his mother, to a Moroccan woman. He had a daughter by his wife and was working as a kitchen designer in Gaithersburg at the time of his arrest.

Through a mutual acquaintance in this tightly knit community, Kwon had met Seifullah Chapman before they encountered each other at the Dar al-Arqam center, where he eventually met fellow group members Abdur-Raheem, Caliph Basha, Idris Surratt, and Ibrahim al-Hamdi.[19] Seifullah was born Randall Blue Chapman in 1972. He had served as a Marine, but was discharged because of a diabetic condition. After his conversion, he made multiple trips to Saudi Arabia—for Hajj in 1996, 1997, 1999, and 2000; he also spent six months in 1998 studying at the Umm al-Qura University in Mecca. He eventually moved to Saudi Arabia in 2002 to teach English. Idris Surratt (born Donald Thomas Surratt II in 1973) was also a convert to Islam and a Marine Corps veteran. He served for approximately three years, which included a stint in Somalia in 1993 where he first learned about and accepted Islam. Surratt was discharged from military service after being shot in the leg during an armed robbery.

One of the most interesting figures convicted in this case is Randall Todd Royer, who took the name Ismail after converting to Islam at the age of nineteen. Royer was born in St. Louis in 1973. He came to the Washington, DC, area in the early 1990s and enrolled in some college classes while also attending the lectures of Jaafar Idris beginning in 1993. Royer worked for the World Assembly of Muslim Youth (WAMY) offices in Northern Virginia for a brief time. Soon after, Royer found himself fighting alongside mujahidin in Bosnia's civil war in the mid-1990s, eventually leaving in 1995 as the conflict was winding down.[20] He returned to the United States in time for the fall 1995 semester at American University in Washington, DC, where he eventually became president of the Muslim Student Association (MSA). Beginning in 1997, he served as Communications Specialist for the Council on American-Islamic Relations (CAIR), among the most high-profile Islamic organizations in the United States. His CAIR profile read: "He served as Washington Bureau Chief for the on-line news site iviews.com, where he wrote investigative pieces on anti-Muslim organizations. . . . He currently writes news releases, speaks with journalists, conducts research, and monitors the media as part of CAIR's media relations effort."[21] Royer was an active blogger, writer, and publisher on Muslim affairs in America, making his arrest and twenty-year sentence all the more shocking for the American Muslim community.[22]

In a move that signaled its initial radicalization, after the group formed, it began meeting more frequently with al-Timimi and Royer, and distancing itself from the local Muslim community.[23] Having established the necessity and religious obligation of preparing for jihad, they met in members' homes and other private locations, keeping the nature of these sessions confidential among the group's members.

COALESCING AROUND SALAFI ISLAM

For the first annual summer camp in July 1994, hosted by the Society for Adherence to the Sunnah, the precursor to Dar al-Arqam, al-Timimi wrote a piece entitled "Reflections: on the Meaning of Our Testimony of Faith." The article read like a classic Salafi manifesto: it covered *al-Wala' wa'l-Bara'* (Love and Hate, or Loyalty and Enmity, for God's sake), the dangers of *shirk* (idolatry), the rejection of tyranny, making *hijra* (emigration) from the lands of infidels, (the sin of) creating law by anything other than the Shari'a, and various forms of hypocrisy.[24] Of course, it also included passages on requirement to "Wage Jihad in the Path of Allah."

Al-Timimi continued to distill this ideology to audiences in the Washington, DC, area during the 1990s as his popularity grew. Ibrahim al-Hamdi was a member of the group who worked at the Islamic Foundation of America (IFA), begun by Saudi Salafists, and was in the United States on a diplomatic visa because his father was a Yemeni diplomat. According to al-Hamdi, al-Timimi knew Safar al-Hawali well, and used to cite his fatwa in support of the 9/11 attacks, reading from the Arabic version to the group. Al-Timimi frequently spoke highly of al-Hawali and referred to him as his shaykh, using some of his fatwas to justify support for the mujahidin in Afghanistan. Additionally, between March and October 2002, Timimi placed dozens of calls to Saudi Arabia to a number belonging to Safar al-Hawali.[25] Al-Timimi also maintained contact with Salman al-'Awda and other Salafi activists in Saudi Arabia.

Al-Timimi traveled to Saudi Arabia in December 2001, and learned of a close association between Shaykh Hammud bin 'Uqla al-Shu'aybi and bin Ladin. The two had maintained communication throughout the early 2000s and Bin 'Uqla authored a fatwa used to justify the 9/11 attacks, "The Eminent Sheikh Humood Bin 'Uqla Ash-Shu'aibi's Statement on the Events that Took Place in America." Searching agents found these materials at Timimi's home, along with other Arabic documents and fatwas by other Saudi clerics. Al-Timimi had also written a four-page document entitled "Suicide Attacks: Are they Suicide? A Sharia Viewpoint." In it, he states that those attacks carried out with good intentions, for the benefit of Islam and Muslims and in order to harm unbelievers, should not be considered suicide in Islam. It went on to say that killing oneself as part of a military operation is permissible under Islam.

Group members were not solely under the influence of Dr. al-Timimi. A representative from the Benevolence International Foundation (BIF) has also contributed to the radicalization of group members. BIF made extensive efforts toward the Salafization of the Chechen conflict (see chapter 5). Yusuf Ansari Wells, BIF representative and fundraiser, showed members of the group jihadi videos from the Qoqaz.net website. One of the group's members, Mahmoud Hasan, attended a presentation by Wells and made a donation to BIF. He later met Wells at another group member's home where they watched jihadi videos. Wells spoke of the Chechen fighters he knew and claimed he was raising funds for orphans and women in Chechnya. According to the indictment of Enaam Arnaout, a BIF official operating in Illinois, "BIF records reveal that its fundraiser Yusuf Ansari Wells openly solicited donations to support *jihad* efforts from various donors. A January 3, 2000, letter to Wells accompanying a money order thanks him for a particular presentation and indicates that the donation is for "our brothers fighting for the sake of Allah" and stating "may Allah continue to help the mujahideen."

A report Wells provided to another BIF employee on May 8, 2001, described an April fundraising trip Wells made to the eastern states on BIF's behalf. Wells's entry for April 9, 2001, discusses a lecture he gave and describes as the main point of his lecture, "That the Taliban are not the bad guys that everybody says they are. And that they have done much good for the establishment of order in the country." The entry for April 15, 2001, discusses Wells's participation in paintball "training" with an elite group and Wells's lecture afterward—"I also stressed the idea of being balanced. That we should not just be jihadis and perfect our fighting skills, but we should also work to perfect our character and strengthen our knowledge of Islam. I also said that Muslims are not just book reading cowards either, and that they should be commended for forming such a group."

ON TO THE TRAINING CAMPS

Clearly, al-Timimi was moved by the condition of Muslims overseas, Afghanistan in particular, and urged his followers to support them. Some members, like Royer, had received paramilitary training in Pakistan's LeT-run camps: "Early in the year 2000, Hamdi learned that a friend of his, Ismail Royer, was planning to attend a LeT training camp in Pakistan. Royer and Hamdi discussed the topic of jihad on a number of occasions and Royer had conveyed to Hamdi his experiences fighting jihad in Bosnia. Hamdi was jealous of Royer and very much wanted to do the same. For a long time, Hamdi has had the desire to go become a mujahidin and die a shahid [martyr]."[26]

Soon after learning of Royer's intentions, al-Hamdi went to visit their mentor, Ali al-Timimi, and privately asked him his opinion and advice regarding going to fight in the jihad and potentially becoming a martyr.[27] Al-Timimi was initially reserved and noncommittal, and prolonged the decision. Hamdi was then studying at the Institute of Islamic and Arabic Science in America (IIASA), the satellite of Ibn Saud Islamic University in Riyadh, Saudi Arabia, based in Fairfax, Virginia. About two weeks later, al-Hamdi approached al-Timimi after he gave a lecture at the American Open University, and again asked him about going to fight with the LeT. Al-Timimi told him that LeT is a good organization, and he had met (LeT founder) Hafiz Saeed's brother at a conference in Britain.[28]

Ismail Royer had attended the LeT camp in Pakistan from January to May 2000. Shortly after Royer's return, at a Friday night lecture at Dar al-Arqam, al-Hamdi asked him for help getting into the LeT camp. Royer agreed, and placed calls from Royer's house to his contacts at LeT in Pakistan making the necessary arrangements for al-Hamdi to attend, which he did for about a month in late August of 2000. Seifullah Chapman would follow in August 2001. All three returned to the United States after completing their training. This training had been made toward the general preparation of jihad, an obligation according to most versions of Salafism. But it did not appear to be in preparation for any specific conflict or campaign; it was done in part through the relationship and admiration al-Timimi had for LeT leader Hafez Saeed, whom he had met at a conference in London.

The preparation had been made, but a time for action had just arrived. On the evening of September 11, 2001, al-Timimi told Yong Ki Kwon to "gather the brothers who own firearms for a meeting, in order to come up with a plan," fearing that there would be an outbreak of anti-Muslim sentiment around the country.[29] In response, Kwon organized a dinner at his home in Fairfax, Virginia, on September 16, 2001, at which al-Timimi told Kwon, Randall Royer, Masoud Khan, Hammad Abdur-Raheem, Caliph Basha, Ibn Abdur-Raheem, Muhammed Aatique, and Khwaja Hasan that the time had come for them to go abroad to join the mujahidin fighting in Afghanistan. During that meeting, he also explicitly stated that American troops, whom he correctly expected to arrive in Afghanistan to fight the Taliban, were legitimate targets for the group. Al-Timimi also instructed the youth at that meeting to seek paramilitary training from LeT in Pakistan—adding that their meeting that night must be kept secret.[30]

In the following days, Kwon, Masoud Khan, and Khwaja Hasan, a Pakistani national who became a U.S. citizen in 1998, went to the Pakistani Embassy in Washington to apply for visas for travel to Pakistan.[31] Aatique purchased tickets for the trip to Pakistan on September 19, 2001, purportedly to visit family and receive treatment for his acne. Al-Timimi had provided them, along with Royer, with instructions on how to reach a LeT training camp undetected. Within a few days, Khan, Hasan, Kwon, and Muhammad Aatique had arrived in Pakistan. In the following weeks, the men had gained entry and begun their training at LeT camps in Muzaffarabad. Meanwhile, in the United States, al-Timimi continued to impress upon the remaining group members the need for training though LeT, and that if they were killed while fighting Americans in Afghanistan, they would die as martyrs.

PAINTBALL GAMES

Over the course of a three-year period leading up to the investigation and their arrests, members of the group played paintball together in order to practice small-unit military tactics, inspired by the idea of becoming mujahidin on a real battlefield, and also repeatedly expressed their desire to die as martyrs in jihad. The paintball training had started in mid-summer 2000 and lasted until September 11, 2001. A fellow Muslim who was not prosecuted in the case had attended the Dar al-Arqam and participated in the paintball activities with the group, and provided the property where they could play paintball games in rural Virginia.

At one point in the training, Hammad Abdur-Raheem and Seiful-lah Chapman established themselves among the group as the paintball "emirs" due to their prior military experience. At certain points in the training, trustworthy members were permitted to shoot live ammunition at a firing range. They also had overnight excursions, where they made encampments in preparation for a time when they might need to fight the government if Muslims were put in government-sponsored holding camps and mosques were shut down.

The paintball games did indeed seem closely tied to militancy in Muslim conflict zones, Chechnya in particular. Some members of the group frequently downloaded videos on jihad from the Qoqaz website, the primary website of the Salafi Chechen resistance. Additionally, the website maintained by the paintball group had links to Islamtoday.com, alsalafyoon.com, qoqaz.net, and islamway.com. In Spring 2003 Caliph Basha told an FBI special agent investigating the case "that paintball was jihad training and that the reason the paintball participants had acquired AK-47-style rifles was that they were the type of weapon used overseas." Hammad Abdur-Raheem, upon learning of this admission, placed a call to Ishmail Royer, which was intercepted. In that call, Abdur-Raheem said that Caliph Basha had "cracked."[32]

The Court Opinion found that Abdur-Raheem intended not to use paintball for "recreation and physical fitness," as he claimed, but instead to prepare for jihad. It also read, "Seifullah Chapman testified that he is a moderate Muslim who does not subscribe to terrorism. He consistently tried to downplay the significance of his involvement in paintball as train-ing for jihad. We found this testimony incredible in light of the consistent testimony of Gharbieh, Thompson, Surratt, Aatique, and Kwon about how intense Chapman was about the training drills and the need for discipline."

Gharbieh testified that Chapman often sang *nasheeds* (war songs praising jihad which the court heard on some of the violent videos in evi-dence) during paintball, and once said that anyone who is going to fight needs to know nasheeds. Kwon also testified that Chapman sang na-sheeds."[33]

Others also testified that Chapman described paintball as a stepping-stone to jihad training camps, and Surratt quoted Chapman as saying, "We're going to learn to fight."[34] There was clear evidence that the group intended to use the paintball training for jihad.

GUNPLAY

In all, thirty-two of the forty-two criminal counts in the indictment against the eleven men pertained to firearms violations. Counts six through twelve of the indictment charged the men with the use of a firearm in the belief that a felony would be committed, while counts thirteen through sixteen and eighteen through forty-one charge members with the use of a firearm in the commission of a crime of violence. Counts eighteen through forty-one cite all but five of the firearms violations as taking place in the eastern United States, predominantly in Virginia.[35]

From 2000 to 2003, the group acquired and/or conducted live-fire training sessions with AK-47 rifles, Saiga .308 rifles, AR-15 rifles, rocket-propelled grenades—and a 12mm antiaircraft gun in October 2001 in Pakistan, used by four of the groups' members—in preparation for waging jihad in Afghanistan alongside the Taliban. While the group members used the heaviest ammunition overseas, the majority of their training involved AK-47s or AK-47-style weapons in the United States. This evidence supports the prosecution's claims that the group intended to use the weapons for a jihad-style attack, as described in the purpose of the paintball training.

Yet, in light of the legally purchased firearms, legal registrations, and NRA memberships, the men also appeared to be gun enthusiasts, especially given the military history of some in the group. Despite the clear threat posed by these group members and others, there still is a lack of evidence pointing to any specific plot to target American civilians or attack American soil with these firearms. The group's primary objective seemed clearly to assist fellow Salafi-jihadi fighters overseas.

■ ■ ■

In al-Timimi's case, his initial da'wa-centered Salafi activism turned into a call to militancy. Here, fellow Muslims involved in overseas conflicts—and the perceived need to come to their aid—led the cleric to instruct his followers to prepare and engage in violent jihad as a necessary part of their faith. The eleven men that made up the group were capable of committing violent acts against Americans or American interests, and were committed to the jihad in speech and action. It is clear they were radicalized largely under Ali al-Timimi's guidance. The American-born cleric had, ultimately, encouraged a select group of his followers to seek jihad training overseas and support Taliban leader Mullah 'Umar.

Although the potential gravity of the group's actions was made manifest in the abundant evidence against it, these individuals under al-Timimi posed less of a threat to domestic security than as added low-level soldiers in the conflict in Afghanistan. The group was clearly enthusiastic about weapons training and the need to prepare for jihad, but also carried out numerous legal firearms activities in their purchases, registrations, and NRA memberships. They were also, per al-Timimi's guidance, highly fearful of reprisals against Muslims in America after 9/11 and even feared they could be rounded up and detained in camps.

The group's primary objective was to assist fellow Salafi-jihadi fighters overseas. Numerous individuals like those in the Virginia Jihad group enlist for a war against the enemy in Islamic lands, "dar al-Islam" (in Kashmir, Afghanistan, Chechnya, etc.), to use the Islamist rhetoric, rather than strike America. Clearly the individuals arrested and sentenced in this case were living in America—many of them American converts to Islam—and had the means to craft a plot against domestic targets. Yet they directed their training and commitment toward foreign conflicts. This need to prepare for jihad in order to defend and fight alongside Muslims overseas is one of the most common points of reference in the literature of Salafi jihadists.

Al-Timimi's close relationship with, and admiration for, Saudi Salafi shaykhs Safar al-Hawali and Salman al-'Awda was one of the clearest indications of his ideological and political affiliations. From them he took religious authority in the form of fatwas to justify training with LeT and preparing for jihad against Americans in Afghanistan. Al-Hawali and al-'Awda, being long-time political activists in Saudi Arabia, had long attempted to reorient Saudi law and society toward their version of the Shari'a. This was conveyed in their communiqués, al-Timimi's study of their writings, and during his trips to Saudi Arabia. In one instance, shortly after the 9/11 attacks, al-Timimi conferred with al-Hawali about writing a letter to the U.S. Congress with the message that the two cultures could coexist. Yet any thought of peaceful coexistence was overruled by persistent enmity toward the presence of American troops in Afghanistan and his outrage over grievances in Muslim lands.

Nine

RADICALIZATION

"Instill in the hearts of your sons the love for Jihad and the love of battlefields."

—Last Will of 'Abdullah 'Azzam

THE FOREMOST PRIORITY of the global Salafi-jihadi movement—that which is behind al-Qaʻida and similarly oriented groups—is to revolutionize Islam. Using the model of past Salafi movements and the teachings of contemporary militant Salafis, they strive to alter Islamic society, to reorient it toward personal and societal codes of law and conduct derived from their reading of early Islamic texts. The term "Salafi" has been used to describe a variety of reformers and activists over the last two centuries, whose work has resulted in a wide range of societal and political ramifications. Throughout colonial occupations and the end of that era, the Salafi movement remained a catalyst for social change, unrest, and turmoil in the Islamic world, ever since it was born out of the Najd in the eastern Arabian desert. In earlier chapters, these Salafi actors from the nineteenth century onward—whose influence spread from the Arabian Peninsula outward—made a call to return to early Islamic ideals within a rigid orthodoxy of religious practices and beliefs.

The twentieth century saw these Salafi ideals transformed into organized political and social movements, notably in Egypt with Hasan al-Banna and Sayyid Qutb, and Abu'l-A'la Mawdudi in Pakistan. In the 1970s, a jihadi movement coalesced around 'Abdullah 'Azzam, as well as around numerous ideologues and guerrilla commanders alike during the jihad against the Soviets. Even after the end of that campaign, however, its supporters continued organizing. Various parts of the movement have since struggled with each other over legitimacy and primacy, many attempting to mobilize a vast Muslim audience into action. And these vying components of the same general movement relied upon much the same doctrine. As Muhammad ibn `Abd al-Wahhab drew heavily on the writings of thirteenth-century Syrian scholar Ibn Taymiyya—using his writings to support arguments for *takfir* (labeling fellow Muslims disbelievers, and making them lawful opponents in warfare)—so too have Salafi-jihadist thinkers and writers throughout the 1990s and 2000s. This entire enterprise, from the beginning, has been a fight against fellow Muslims, and within Islam. That fight has spilled over and foreign enemies of the umma have been attacked; such attacks are not just against the United States, but against a wide swath of countries from Southeast Asia to Russia, from Africa to western Europe.

The role of Salafi activists in the United States in radicalizing American Muslims has been largely underexplored. Although the majority of the activists, who began organizing the Muslim community in the 1960s, and their descendants have been nonviolent, they nonetheless established Salafi Islam as normative, and laid the ideological groundwork for Salafi-jihadi activists. More broadly speaking, Salafi-oriented groups in the United States have found success by establishing themselves as authorities on Islam in their communities and sometimes nationwide. Without a doubt, Salafi currents have swayed popular Muslim culture in America. The most popular Muslim American clerics were largely educated in Mecca or Medina, or have other educational links to the official Saudi Salafi establishment. And as noted in previous chapters, the funding and organizational efforts to spread that form of Salafi Islam were immense. As some of those Salafi currents transplanted in America have focused on Muslims in crisis zones over the last two decades, so have they inspired a consciousness about the need to act on behalf of those fellow believers. That action came in the form of urging charitable giving, educating fellow Muslims about the plight of their brothers and sisters living under states of oppression or occupation, or preparing to physically train for combat. In its most extreme cases, calls for action led adherents to form terrorist plots independently, selecting targets whose attack they believed would benefit the cause of Islam.

It is clear there are radical, violent strands within Salafism, but not every Salafi is militant. A categorical denunciation of all Salafis as violent or militant clearly misses the mark; ideology, belief, and doctrine are nuanced, and calls for action are varied. Yet, across the Muslim world, organized campaigns of violence have been carried out—the vast majority of times by Salafis or those influenced by their ideology. For the numerous governments seeking to combat that ideology, it is necessary to examine the radicalization of both Muslim communities and individual Muslims, while paying close attention to the role of ideology. While there have been many attempts to decipher the radicalization process, many overlook the overarching role of ideology in guiding activist movements, from the top down. Along those lines, a model for radicalization can be suggested that broadly describes the experiences of individual Muslims, small groups of like-minded believers, and larger activist circles.

FOUR STAGES OF RADICALIZATION

People rarely wake up one morning and decide to arbitrarily commit an act of violence, and Salafi-jihadi militancy is no exception. Muslims are brought into violent jihadi campaigns after a deliberate study of doctrine and ideology, the final step being the individual's affirmation of belief that violence is a necessary component of defending the *umma* and raising the word of God for the cause of establishing His Shari'a on earth. The following model of activist radicalization cannot attempt to describe the phenomenon of Salafi militancy from its inception; it focuses instead on the radicalization of Muslims from the 1990s onward, with an emphasis on Islamist radicalization in the West. Intentionally, socioeconomic indicators are absent in this model. Profiles from radicalization cases depict Muslims from a range of family backgrounds, classes, ethnicities, and education and income levels; Salafi-jihadi ideology clearly forms the common factor among them. Accordingly, a majority of these cases of jihadi radicalization occur over the following four stages:

1. Introduction to the movement and its literature;
2. Immersion in Salafi thinking and mindset;

3. Growing dissatisfaction or frustration with a lack of results or perceived inaction;
4. Resolve to receive training; individual is resolved in action by the
   principle of preparation for jihad.

These steps reflect the distinct changes in attitude and worldview a
potential mujahid goes through before arriving at the point where he or
she is prepared and intent upon jihad. This model focuses on events and
influences that lead to jihadi activism; it leaves off where one resolves to
carry out a terrorist act, or join the mujahidin overseas in combat. There
does appear to be a "line of militancy" between the third and fourth stage,
where one crosses over from nonviolent to violent intent. It stands to
reason, then, that intervention would have the best odds of success in the
earlier stages of radicalization.

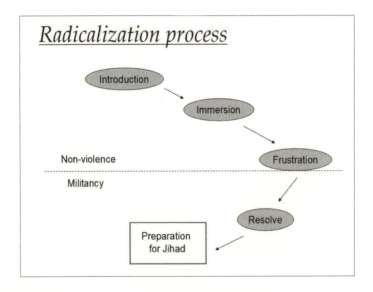

In the first stage of radicalization, a subject comes into contact with
the movement through one of many paths to radicalization, such as videos or audio lectures, online articles or magazines, Salafi practitioners at
mosques, Islamic centers or conferences, or through other forms of outreach. They lead the individual down a path of study in Salafi Islam. This
often includes a series of essential readings 'aqida (doctrine), typically
embodying the teachings of Muhammad ibn 'Abd al-Wahhab. It is some-

times a part of a formal education program with structured coursework, or it can take the form of individuals piecing together their own Salafist education from the ample supply of published literature. The majority of Sunni Muslims who encounter this literature do not heed the call to Salafi activism; they remain unmoved by it or defer to the traditions of other schools of thought (Hanafi, Shafi'i, Maliki, Hanbali). Some, for a variety of reasons, will pursue further learning, often through a shaykh under whom they can study; or they may enter into a community of believers or an educational program.

In the second stage, the individual or collective immerses itself in the thinking and mindset of Salafi Islam. Depending on the branch of the movement one embraces, this may or may not include exposure to the culture of jihad that surrounds militant Salafism. The degree to which one aligns with militant ideologues is predictive of one's trajectory toward violence. This stage can last anywhere from a matter of months to several years. During this period, the individual becomes increasingly consumed in the doctrine of the movement, seeing the world in terms of black and white: *haram* (forbidden) and *halal* (permissible), *kufr* (disbelief or heresy) and *iman* (belief), *shirk* (polytheism) and *tawhid* (monotheism). During this transformation stage, the individual embarks upon the application of learned principles and forges a plan for action based on his or her perceived state of Muslim affairs, and of the world and their place in it. After sufficient study and mastery of the doctrine, an individual on this path typically looks to spread this message to his fellow Muslims, in order to bring the umma back to "true" Islamic practices. This outreach can be done in a number of ways, and the circle of Salafism they orbit will largely determine an individual's activism. For some this will translate into fundraising or charitable work, for some educating or community organizing, and for others it may mean seeking to support the mujahidin, through word or deed.

For those Muslims brought up from a young age (typically teenage years) by a Salafi shaykh or institution, this process is more uniform. The individual comes away from their formative education with the worldview of their shaykh or institution. For *da'wa*-oriented Salafis, some will find disillusionment with nonviolent activism, and gravitate toward more radical messages. The third stage is most applicable to those Salafi activists who entered the movement primarily as nonviolent practitioners. It is marked by growing dissatisfaction or frustration with inaction, as the individual attempts (but often fails) to spread the message they have embraced and bring other Muslims' worldviews in line with their own. While a number of individuals who embrace the Salafi movement never move beyond such nonviolent tactics, those who have carried out an attack, joined a training camp, or attempted a terrorist plot, did, by and large, find the inactive Islam of their fellow Muslims—even fellow Salafis—to be inadequate. Theirs is characterized by a constant search for the "true Islam," persistently seeing others as falling short of the model of the *Salaf* (the pious predecessors, for which the movement is named).

In the fourth and final stage, the individual resolves to join the mujahidin in their battle against oppression and tyranny. Often, in accordance with their Salafi training, they seek out a trusted brother who can bring them to a training camp or provide the guidance to carry out an attack. For the Virginia Jihad Group discussed in the previous chapter, this took place largely under the tutelage of 'Ali al-Timimi. A select group of followers determined to pursue violent means as al-Timimi and other Salafi ideologues in their circle taught believers that such actions were obligatory to their faith. Other cases of radicalized groups such as those in the Yemeni community in Lackawanna, New York, a group of seven men in Portland, Oregon, and the young men in New Jersey who plotted to attack the Fort Dix Army Base were inspired by the same militant Salafi message that al-Timimi espoused, but with far less direct contact with their imam and absent the formal learning setting.

An interesting component, if perhaps anecdotal, in this final stage of the radicalization process is the presence of some emotional or traumatic event in the second or third stage that leaves the individual feeling that he or she has nothing left to lose. This was the case for John Walker Lindh and Adam Gadahn, as well as at least one of the Duka brothers who were part of the Fort Dix plot. For some, the radicalization process can be brief. Certain individuals seem to be more predisposed toward violence or radical action to bring about results. These individuals are more receptive to the militant message and effectively dismiss nonviolent forms of activism like political or social organizing. This was the case for Harun Fazul, the Comoran al-Qa`ida operative, and converts like Adam Gadahn, who spent a few short months studying Salafi doctrine and practice before demonstrating an inclination to participate in jihadi operations. Clearly, there is much diversity within the samples that inform the above four-stage model, and outliers to be sure. Not all will pass through four distinct stages before accepting the principle of jihadi preparation, and certainly not on uniform trajectories. But the model does help demonstrate how important a factor ideology is in producing violent activism.

PATHS TO RADICALIZATION

In the first, introductory step, individuals begin down a path to radicalization that can result in an immersion into jihadi culture and a determination to carry out an act of violence in furtherance of their cause. Jihad is not the ultimate goal of the militant Salafi movement. Their foremost objective is to bring fellow Muslims to a Salafi reading of Islam and, from that point, to deliver salvation to the global Muslim community by returning it to the "true Islam." These efforts are manifest through various pieces of Salafi literature, videos, speeches, and other materials introduced at the mosque, in prison, or online.

The literature from the Salafi-jihadi movement began arriving on the Internet in the 1990s, as the Afghan jihad against the Soviets drew to a close. This took place largely through the efforts of the Afghan veterans from the 1970s, who took on the role of emissaries, bringing the message of the mujahidin's victory to their home countries; through scholars, local mosques, *madrasas*, and various media outlets, they called on Muslims to aid their brothers living under oppression and/or occupation. Beginning in the late 1990s, the CIA and other intelligence agencies began to actively monitor the nascent community of jihadi websites and discussion forums. For the bulk of that decade, most materials were in Arabic, with sporadic translations available. In the latter part of the 2000s, these magazines and articles began becoming widely available in English, making them accessible to Muslims in the West, as well as English speakers in the non-Arab world. This medium introduced the writings of `Abd Allah `Azzam, Sayyid Qutb, and other late revolutionary Islamist leaders, as well as contemporary Salafi ideologues like Abu Muhammad al-Maqdisi and Abu Basir al-Tartusi to a new generation of young Muslims.

There is a strong and growing online readership of militant Salafi ideology, and a number of domestic U.S. cases have demonstrated how "homegrown" terrorists can be inspired to act through this body of jihadi literature. Websites like Tawhed.ws (which is maintained by Abu Muhammad al-Maqdisi) have long provided one of the largest collections of militant Salafi and jihadi literature available online. Readers find sprawling collections of writings from Salafi ideologues, thinkers, and commanders across the globe (along with an expansive readership in both Arabic and English, which came available circa 2008–2009). The bulk of this literature focuses on the explanation and implementation of the Shari`a, and related subsets of the topic. Nearly all Salafi scholars object to Muslims living under apostate laws and political systems—such as democracy, or any man-made law—transgressing the law that God has decreed. Within the framework, scholars such as al-Maqdisi, Abu Qatada al-Filistini, and Abu Basir al-Tartusi enjoy tremendous credibility as leading resistance figures, and are among the most widely read.[1] All have strong Salafi credentials and have been prolific writers and leading voices in the movement; they have also been imprisoned or exiled from their homeland. They are perceived as being true to Islam for placing the interests of Muslims before themselves, which makes them sincere, legitimate, and incorruptible. For the mujahidin, they enjoy the status of scholarly authorities.

The Internet plays another distribution role, of course, for jihadi videos and communiqués. A number of separate, quasi-affiliated media entities produce recruiting, motivational, instructional, and strategic videos for al-Qa`ida and affiliated jihadi groups. Since the early 2000s, the production quality and distribution capabilities of these videos have increased steadily, and audiences have come to expect slick production values, often with the newscast feel of al Jazeera. In the Fort Dix case in May 2006, group members were highly motivated by jihadi videos they found online. Mohamad Shnewer, the only one of the six who spoke and read Arabic, downloaded numerous videos by al-Sahab media productions, which has been the primary media producer for al-`Qa`ida's central command in the Afghanistan-Pakistan border region. Shnewer was a vigorous proponent of these jihadi videos—particularly those featuring attacks against U.S. military personnel—distributing them to fellow members of the group and others with whom they met.[2] This case, like the foiled 2006 U.K. plan to down ten transatlantic airliners, demonstrates how groups of young men with little or no contact with formal terrorist groups can be inspired by Salafi literature and jihadi videos found online.

THE MAGAZINE CRAZE

Beginning in 2002, two magazines from Saudi Arabia set an example for the publication of comprehensive doctrinal and military training literature. *Sawt al-Jihad* (The Voice of Jihad) and *Mu`askar al-Battar* (the al-Battar training camp, named for the late commander and strategist Yusuf al-`Uyayri) published monthly issues for just under two years.[3] Al-`Uyayri, who took the nom de guerre *al-Battar*, or "cutting edge," was a Saudi-born mujahid and veteran of the anti-Soviet jihad killed in 2003 by Saudi security forces. *Al-Battar* magazine focused on paramilitary training. It featured techniques on urban warfare, basic weapons training and maintenance, bomb making, and other topics from commanders who fought in various campaigns in Afghanistan, Saudi Arabia, the Balkans, and elsewhere. In lengthy detail, these authors laid out explicit instructions regarding security measures, operational guidelines, cell organization, and communications.

Sawt al-Jihad, meanwhile, featured ideological justifications for jihad, in politically charged, anti-U.S. articles from leading Salafi-jihadi leaders and strategists. It also produced other content for the mujahidin, such as poems, testimonials and stories of martyrs. Together, *Sawt al-Jihad* and *Mu`askar al-Battar* were forerunners of scores of other online magazines in the years to come. Initially, many of those magazines copied their format, layout, and content. For example, they spawned *Majjalat al-Fath* (Magazine of the Conquest) and *Dhurwat al-Sanam* (The Pinnacle) in Iraq; *Majallat al-Ansar* (Magazine of the Partisans), *Tora Bora,* and *al-Hassad* (The Harvester) in Afghanistan. In Yemen, the al-Qa`ida branch composed of Yemenis and displaced Saudi members began publishing *Sada al-Malahim* (The Echo of Battles) in early 2009. Others have continued to spawn as well out of this organic magazine enterprise, such as *Sada al-Jihad* (The Echo of Jihad), published by the Global Islamic Media Front, putting out tons of robust and slick monthly issues in the late 2000s.

These online periodicals from various fronts of jihad were part of a
rapid growth in jihadi materials online that occurred in the early 2000s.
Ironically, this took place largely alongside a worldwide surge of interest
in jihad and jihadi materials following 9/11. This was demonstrated in the
expanded readership of Internet discussion forums on jihad and militant
Salafi Islam, greater readership of websites with Salafi and jihadi librar-
ies like tawhed.ws, and a general increase in the quantity and quality of
media output from al-Qa`ida and like-minded groups.

DEVELOPMENT OF AN ONLINE CURRICULUM

Archives of *Sawt al-Jihad*, *Mu`askar al-Battar*, *Dhurwat al-Sanam*, and
all the other subsequent magazines have provided a rich body of online
content. Efforts were made within the jihadi community to extract articles from these publications and create collections that could be used
as training curriculum for aspiring mujahidin. Not all of these collections
came from a single source, and some encouraged cells to organize and
operate independently under their guidelines while others encouraged
recruits to join existing jihadi groups for additional training and guidance,
in order to avoid attacks that might damage the public image of the movement. At the same time, encyclopedias on jihad with content from an
array of sources—including excerpts from U.S. military and intelligence
training manuals—became available online. From at least 2003 onward,
the expansive *Encyclopedia of Preparation* (*Mawsu`at al-`Idad*), the *Encyclopedia of Jihad* (*Mawsu`at al-Jihad*)—prepared by the mujahidin
in Afghanistan—and other virtual "encyclopedias," as they styled themselves, were published and distributed online.[4]

Additional encyclopedias have emerged, for example the *Encyclopedia of Periodicals and Publications on Jihad*, containing dozens of files
and links to magazines, mostly published in 2002–2003. It is described
as a presentation and explanation of the mujahidin's communications,
made available to all Muslims. Its contents include a video course and
seven-part audio course from (captured) jihadi strategist Abu Mus`ab al-
Suri, who calls for organized resistance. Additionally, the encyclopedia
includes the writings of `Abdullah `Azzam; content from jihadi periodicals
and publications such as *Sawt al-Jihad* and *al-Battar*, statements from

Usama bin Ladin, courses on security precautions; responses to criticism of the mujahidin and the jihad movement; poetry in praise of jihad; and war videos.

Such encyclopedias illustrate how the community of mujahidin and their supporters not only develop and distribute curriculum for the aspiring, inexperienced youth who wish to join their ranks, but also consolidate jihadi strategy and serve as a conduit for implementing that strategy within the lowest ranks—those Arab and Muslim youth who browse this content and contemplate taking action. Moreover, according to al-Suri and other jihadi leaders and strategists, the mujahidin should have a thorough understanding of correct Islamic belief and doctrine (in accordance with Salafi Islam), before moving on to any weapons or combat training. Indeed, ideology is more often than not a fundamental prerequisite for joining the mujahidin, and one finds that captured or repentant mujahidin all progressed along a path of ideological radicalization until they eventually sought armed combat in support of the cause.

AT THE MOSQUE

Few mosques in the West have openly promoted militancy in the years following 9/11. However, mosques provide a meeting place for Muslims, some of whom, naturally, have more radical views than their leaders; these individuals often gravitate toward one another and form groups parallel to the mosque. The Virginia Jihad Group was an example of individuals coming together at a small Islamic center (which maintained a prayer space within its rented office complex) through shared beliefs and worldview. They were under the instruction of 'Ali al-Timimi, but hundreds, or perhaps thousands, of other Muslims had also heard his lectures. In that case, and a number of others, the militant training they undertook for jihad overseas was kept clandestine and withheld from other Muslims in the community.

Aside from this gravitational pull of hard-line elements at the mosque around which others of a like mind revolve, there have been cases where a terrorist plot originated within a mosque. Two al-Qa'ida members, Juma al-Dosari (a Saudi Imam) and Kamal Derwish (a Yemeni born in Lackawanna, raised in Saudi Arabia), began giving informal talks at the Lackawanna mosque, near Buffalo in upstate New York. Although some in the community were concerned about the militant tone the two carried in their sermons, the two nonetheless used the mosque as a meeting and recruiting ground until they made plans to attend training camps in Afghanistan.[5]

THROUGH THE PRISON SYSTEM

Prisons in the United States (New York State in particular) essentially hosted an extensive presence of militant Salafi Muslims during the late 1980s and 1990s, as many officials were unaware of the ideological framework of terrorist groups. These inmates were radicalized—and in some cases recruited by terrorist groups—while serving their prison terms. According to the testimony of then–FBI Assistant Director for Counterterrorism John Pistole, "convicted terrorists from the 1993 World Trade Center bombing were put into their prisons' general population where they radicalized inmates and told them that terrorism was part of Islam."[6]

Even more troubling, a systematic militant Islamist radicalization was taking place in the New York State Department of Corrections under its own chaplain, Warith Deen Umar. According to Pistole, "Umar denied prisoners access to mainstream imams and materials. He sought to incite prisoners against America, preaching that the 9/11 hijackers should be remembered as martyrs and heroes. Umar has since been banned from ever entering a New York State prison."[7]

Violent plots were even hatched within prison walls. Inside the maximum-security Folsom State Prison outside Sacramento, California, Kevin James and his cellmate created a group called Jama`at al-Islam al-Sahih (The Association of True Islam) in 1997.[8] The two recruited as many as a dozen other inmates, who drafted plans to carry out explosives attacks against U.S. government, military, and Jewish targets in the Los Angeles area. James also provided detailed instructions for group members outside prison, and envisioned an organization that would also play a role in "correcting" the Islamic practices of the American Muslim community, evident from his letters. Salafi ideology—as demonstrated in James' writings and guidance to the group—was paramount; he had become versed in Islamic jurisprudence and supported his argument for armed struggle based on "evidence" he provided from early Islamic sources. Cell members, who had pledged an oath of loyalty (bay`a) to James, were robbing gas stations to finance the group when they were arrested in 2005. Neither authorities in the FBI nor the California Department of Corrections were previously aware of the group.

SALAFI RADICALIZATION AMONG CONVERTS

Three prominent cases of Americans converting to jihad show that converts generally make increasingly radical Salafi contacts after an initial introduction and interest in the movement. These three, John Walker Lindh, Adam Gadahn, and Daniel Maldonado, were all teenage American converts to Islam who identified with the message of resistance they found online, and then at the mosque. The young men's reading and postings on discussion forums soon after converting show that they were attracted to the purity of Salafi Islam.

John Walker Lindh

John Walker Lindh inquired about Islam and the requirements of becoming a Muslim on chat rooms, and began using the screen name "Brother Mujahid." He developed some rudimentary Salafi beliefs from online contacts, which led him to reject the first mosque he sought to visit as "unorthodox." As we know, Lindh sought an almost mythically pure Islam, traveling from California to Yemen, then to Pakistan, and ultimately to Afghanistan where he found what he was seeking among the mujahidin fighting Coalition forces. Yet, Lindh's radicalization occurred in California. Subsequent encounters only bolstered his Salafi beliefs, which eventually turned to militancy. A signal of his early Salafi beliefs came when he was first searching for a mosque to pray in—and make his conversion—and he rejected the first mosque he visited as unorthodox.[9] This obsession with outward compliance with the *Shari`a* (Islamic law) is a hallmark of the Salafi sect.

Lindh, as well as Gadahn and Maldonado, seemed to accrue increasingly radical contacts as he ventured into Islam. His first contacts online appear to be Salafis primarily concerned with implementation of the Shari`a. He then became close to Tabligh-i-Jamaat members (not Salafi itself, but these contacts were ideologically close in nature to Salafi Islam) active in missionary work in the western United States He persistently gravitated toward (sometimes militant) Salafis—in the United States, in Yemen, and ultimately in northwestern Pakistan and Afghanistan.

After Lindh returned for a summer break from his studies in Yemen, he learned that his parents were divorced and his father declared that he was gay. John did not again speak of this, and arrived in Pakistan via Sana'a, en route to Afghanistan, a few months later.

Adam Gadahn

At age seventeen, Adam Yahiye Gadahn converted to Islam at the Islamic Society of Orange County, witnessed by the mosque's imam. Soon after he got a job as night watchman at that mosque, but was fired for sleeping on the job. Within a few months, in early 1996, he was under the tutelage of two al-Qa`ida recruiters, Khalil al-Deek and Hisham Diab. He began wearing traditional Arab dress akin to that of Gulf Salafis. Gadahn was effectively under their control; the two men often referred to him as their "little rabbit."

Like Lindh, he had done much Salafi reading online and was pre-pared to convert—and also knew the type of Islam he was looking for—as soon as he arrived at the mosque. He spent roughly one year studying Salafi Islam, first at the mosque on his own, and then with Diab and Deek, before he left for Pakistan on orders from, and at the expense of, the two al-Qa`ida recruiters. He returned to California a few months later ill and underweight. His grandfather, Carl Pearlmann, helped care for him in their home in California. After his grandfather's death, Gadahn returned to Pakistan permanently, and has since been featured in a number of al-Qa`ida videos and serves as a lieutenant to Ayman al-Zawahiri.

Daniel Maldonado

Daniel Maldonado, who called himself Daniel al-Jughaifi, pleaded guilty in April 2007 to joining al-Qa`ida and training in camps run by the Islamic Courts Union, which sought to establish an Islamic state in Somalia.[10] Incarcerated at age twenty-eight, he was given a ten-year prison sentence for receiving training from a terrorist organization. Born in a suburb out-side Boston, Daniel Maldonado dropped out of high school and moved from his native Massachusetts to a Muslim enclave in Houston soon after his conversion, hoping to find sanctuary from his perceived persecution of Muslims in America. At that same time, he became active on a U.S.-based Salafi website. He served as a webmaster for Islamicnetworking.

org, delving into increasingly hard-line topics in his postings. However, he was dissatisfied with the inaction of his brothers, and moved to Cairo in search of a place to practice "true" Islam.

Maldonado initially chose to travel to Egypt in November 2005 to continue his Islamic studies among a community of believers after he had previously expressed grievances against Muslim persecution in the United States. But upon arriving in Cairo, he elected to take residence in Alexandria, where he enrolled at the Qortoba center. In his blogs from Egypt, Daniel Maldonado describes "neo-salafis" expelled from a local Alexandria mosque for bringing the bickering and discord of Cairo, complaining of Cairene Salafis' incessant debate. There is no evidence that he sought to join any particular militant group in the country. Rather, his online postings show that he was becoming more deeply immersed in the texts of Salafism, such as the writings of Muhammad Ibn 'Abd al-Wahhab.

In a post on his personal blog, danielaljughifi.wordpress.com, he writes about his obsession with works by Ibn 'Abd al-Wahhab, the eponymous founder of the Wahhabi movement, members of which typically label themselves as Salafi or *Muwahhidun* (monotheists) rather than Wahhabists. On May 19, 2006, he wrote, "Seeing that I have always been a lover of the books and writings of Sheikhul Islam Muhammad Ibn Abdul Wahab(r) I would start with his books. After getting a few I some what became obsessed and went on a rampage trying to buy anything and everything he or his grandsons wrote [sic]."

Yet Daniel was not a Salafi of the Saudi establishment, calling them *tabdi'i*, meaning they frequently label other Muslims' practices "innovations," which by their nature lead to sin, according to Salafi ideology.[11] Commenting on 'Abdullah al-Faisal, who was imprisoned for nine years for encouraging British Muslims to attend jihadi training camps, Daniel wrote, "He explanes the groups and there deviancies and this is where he mentioned the 'Saudi Salafis' and made Takfeer of them. I do not care for the 'Salafis' niether, with their extra Tabde'e attitude and all But I think that Takfeer on them is a bit extreme [sic]." At this time, only a few months before he left for Somalia, he apparently believed that *takfir,* or labeling other Muslims as infidels, was an extreme belief.

Arrested by Kenyan authorities after he fled from Kismaayo, he told his interviewers that he left Egypt to participate in the jihad in Somalia, describing it as "raising the word of Allah, uppermost, by speaking and fighting against all those who are against the Islamic State."[12] After deciding to join the jihad, he believed he "would be fighting the Somali militia, and that turned into fighting the Ethiopians, and if Americans came, I would fight them too." According to transcripts presented by the FBI in the criminal complaint, he also said he would "kill other Muslims, in an attack, if they were apostates and not faithful Muslims." This statement contradicted his earlier postings criticizing takfir, as he was apparently now willing to kill fellow Muslims for religious deviations.

Maldonado's route to jihad in fact began in the United States and online, and was continued in Alexandria. Both before and after his time in Egypt, Maldonado was primarily concerned with the affairs of the umma (in particular the Muslim community depicted by Salafi ideologues), and the future direction of Islam, as his postings illustrate. He continued to immerse himself as much as possible in Islam, and specifically in the doctrines of the Salafiyya, and he sought out such instruction in Alexandria. After a year there, Maldonado moved toward more militant Salafi activists, ultimately finding his way to an al-Qa'ida-linked training camp in Somalia after leaving Alexandria in November 2006.

After arriving in Egypt, Daniel Maldonado was already a dedicated Salafi and soon after opted to join the mujahidin. His initial radicalization occurred, like Lindh' and Gadahn', largely online, which then led to Salafi contacts at local mosques, overseas, and ultimately to the mujahidin. These cases—and many others in Europe, North Africa, Southeast Asia, and elsewhere—show a ladder of increasingly radical Salafi contacts leading up to the point of enlisting with the mujahidin. At some point along the path, each individual broke with the nonviolent Salafis that introduced him or her to the movement, seeing them as insufficiently dedicated.

As was the case with Lindh and Gadahn, Maldonado converted and displayed an immediate interest in Salafism. They were all persistently unsatisfied with the Salafi Islam practiced in the United States They both sought more "pure" or "correct" Islam, culminating in participation in training and limited armed conflict with mujahidin fighting alongside al-Qa'ida members. Individuals who find the Islam of the Saudi Salafi establishment to be incorrect, hypocritical, etc., often pursue the teachings of more radical Salafis who endorse jihad and the active creation of an Islamic state. That transition marks a point of departure from nonviolence; but in terms of Islamic doctrine, their beliefs are largely the same—it is a difference over the correct response to Western influence and oppression of Muslims.

In the three cases discussed above, all discovered Islam online, read the literature, and partook in discussion forums, and all were seeking out various forms of resistance. Similar to the Fort Dix group, Gadahn, Maldonado, and Lindh all began observing a strict adherence to the Shari`a, in particular the outward aspects, such as adopting Arab or traditional Muslim dress, growing beards, and forbidding music, ornamentation, or photographs in the mosque. Throughout the immersion stage, they routinely confronted or attempted to correct other Muslims' perceived errors, and often found mosques they attended to be inadequately Islamic.

Each of these individuals gravitated toward the black-and-white rigidity of Salafi Islam, arriving at the mosque with literal and strict interpretations of the Shari`a already in place. From there, they pursued increasingly radical contacts, and further immersed themselves in militant Salafi ideology. Finally, they adopted the doctrine of jihad as an obligation for Muslims, and sought training to carry it out. Through the various paths to radicalization described here, it is clear that Salafi doctrine provides the ideological basis for jihadi radicalization. And through a variety of means and media, this movement strives to bring other Muslims to a Salafi reading of Islam. Not merely the jihadi rhetoric of Usama bin Ladin and other such leaders, but educational, charitable, and missionary organizations tied to Salafi Islam play a pivotal role in this process, solidifying the image of Salafi Islam as pure and unadulterated by modernity and innovation.

Ten

THE TREND CONTINUES

SALAFI IDEOLOGY HAS evolved greatly in the two-and-a-half centuries since its formal inception as a movement. In the late eighteenth century, it emerged as a religious reform movement, focused on "correcting" the doctrine and practice of Muslims, primarily in eastern Arabia. Muhammad Ibn ʿAbd al-Wahhab's ideas remained salient, and a broader reform movement spread from his doctrine and the body of ideas from earlier Islamic scholars upon which it was based. As this ideology was infused into disparate parts of the Islamic community, it was transformed repeatedly, and was often an engine for Islamic thought and discussion.

In the nineteenth century Jamal al-Din al-Afghani popularized the term "Salafi" as the name of his reform movement, taking it far beyond the original precepts that defined the movement in Arabia. Publishing from Paris along with his close associate Muhammad ʿAbduh in the 1880s, al-Afghani debated ideas of philosophy, science, and religion among Parisian intellectual circles. This Salafi trend was not to last, however, and upon its return to Egypt with ʿAbduh and subsequent reformers, the movement refocused on religious practices and an effort to shed the decadence of modernity that contaminated Muslim society. The Egyptian reformer Rashid Rida played a key role in reconciling the original ideas and doctrine of Ibn ʿAbd al-Wahhab with the contemporary trends of Salafism that were predominant in the early twentieth century.

The most significant development of Salafi thought, doctrine, and activism—at least in terms of contemporary militancy and the jihadi movement—came during the tumult of the 1950s and 60s in Egypt. As the continually growing Islamist movement in Egypt confronted the political regime, challenging it over the very basis of law upon which the society was based, their social organizing and mobilization gave way to radical, militant means of implementing their vision of society. Displaced Islamist activists from Egypt found a place in Saudi educational institutions, and a new ideological hybrid was born. The ideology brewed in Saudi universities in the late 1950s and 1960s was thus actively spread throughout the world by Saudi Arabian funding and myriad influential organizations like the Muslim World League and its charitable, financial, and da'wa subsidiaries.

The core precepts that have defined the Salafi movement over these centuries are still advocated for today by a wide range of scholars and activists. This movement has been about identity in a modern setting: defending against the decay in civilization after the end of the Prophet's era. The modern-day followers of Salafism, especially those in the West, need affirmation of their identity in a period where Islam is estranged from the predominant culture of society. Currently, English-speaking ideologues increasingly provide an avenue into the movement, with clerics such as the Yemeni-American Anwar al-Awlaqi showing their influence via connections to a number of terrorist acts against the United States.

Anwar al-Awlaqi was born in New Mexico in 1971. His father, who hailed from the Awlaq tribe that dominated much of Shabwah Province in eastern Yemen, had come to the United States to earn a degree in agricultural economics.[1] He would eventually become agricultural minister in Yemen. Anwar spent his early years in the States, but returned with his father to their native Yemen where he spent his teenage years. In 1991 he returned to the United States to pursue an engineering degree at Colorado State University.[2] After graduation, he became a leader at a local mosque in Fort Collins, Colorado, and soon afterward at an Islamic center in San Diego, where he was also working toward a master's degree in education.

In 1996 Anwar led San Diego's Masjid al-Ribat al-Islami, and served as imam there for four years. In 1998–99, al-Awlaqi served as vice president for a charity founded by the influential Yemeni Islamist figure 'Abd al-Majid al-Zindani, of the Charitable Society for Social Welfare, Inc. Federal prosecutors have described that charity as a front used to finance al-Qa'ida and Usama bin Ladin.[3] But during his years in San Diego, al-Awlaqi also made contacts with Khalid al-Mihdhar and Nawaf al-Hazmi, two of the 9/11 hijackers. While the two did speak to al-Awlaqi and attended his lectures, it seems unlikely he was aware of their plot. But even before 9/11, al-Awlaqi drew the attention of federal investigators over his involvement with al-Zindani's charity. In early 2001, al-Awlaqi moved to the northern Virginia area, taking up a position as imam at the Dar al-Hijrah mosque, one of the largest in the area. The mosque was also a regular place of worship for al-Midhar, al-Hazmi, and another hijacker, Hani Hanjour. During his time in the northern Virginia area, al-Awlaqi also served for a time as Muslim chaplain at George Washington University.[4] In 2002 he left the country for the United Kingdom, where he went on a lecture tour over the course of several months, giving numerous talks that drew Muslim youth in particular. But before moving to Yemen, al-Awlaqi returned briefly to the northern Virginia area where he met with Ali al-Timimi and allegedly discussed the matter of recruiting young Muslims for jihadi campaigns abroad.[5] Al-Awlaqi was also close to other prominent, militant Salafis, including 'Umar 'Abd al-Rahman (the imprisoned "blind shaykh"). In mid-2006, al-Awlaqi was arrested by Yemeni authorities (roughly two years after he resettled in Yemen with his wife and children) and detained for eighteen months. Al-Awlaqi said FBI agents repeatedly interrogated him during that time regarding his ties to the hijackers.

Al-Awlaqi lectures found a strong audience, particularly on the Internet. His writings have shown up on the computers of numerous jihadi suspects, and are widely circulated on jihadi message forums and websites. Much of his appeal lies in the fact that he is a flawless and compelling speaker (in English as well as Arabic), and can reach an English-speaking Muslim audience while maintaining the credibility of one possessing the mastery of Qur'anic Arabic. Prototypical of militant Salafis, he claimed the world was nearing a confrontation between the West and the mujahidin, and Muslims would need to choose sides. Giving support to the insurgents in Iraq and Palestinian suicide bombers, he spoke of the Muslim world being in a state of siege.

A number of terrorism cases in the United Kingdom and Canada uncovered transcripts and audio files of al-Awlaqi promoting the military strategies of the late Saudi al-Qa'ida commander Yusuf al-'Uyayri.[6] On his website, www.anwar-alawlaki.com, he published, among other articles, "44 Ways to Support the Jihad," an English-language (and updated) version of the well-known treaty *39 Ways to Support the Jihad*. One of those convicted in the Fort Dix plot in New Jersey, Shain Duka, raved about al-Awlaqi's talks. He told fellow members of his group, "You gotta hear this lecture . . . the truth, no holds barred, straight how it is!"[7] Al-Awlaqi came to the forefront of media attention in late 2009, when his e-mail conversations with Maj. Nidal Malik Hasan, the army psychiatrist who killed thirteen people at the Fort hood Army Base in Texas, came to light. Al-Awlaqi praised Hasan's actions as a courageous act of defiance. Al-Awlaqi was also a figure in the radicalization of a Minnesota Somali man, Mohamoud Hassan, who in November 2008 gave up a university education to enlist in al-Shabaab training camps in Somalia. He too had listened to audio lectures by the Islamist Yemeni cleric Anwar al-Awlaqi.[8] Less than two months after the Fort Hood shootings, al-Awlaqi came to the media's attention again, this time for his contacts with the Nigerian man who lived in Yemen and attempted to blow up an airliner arriving in Detroit on Christmas Day, 2009.

Al-Awlaqi is indeed a critical figure in Salafist radicalization, particularly for the audience of English-speaking Muslims. However, he is one of a number of clerics spreading their message on Internet forums, through media distribution outlets online, and in lecture venues and Islamic centers. Among this group of Salafi preachers and ideologues, there is a circle of militant Salafists advocating violent jihad as the necessary means of establishing an Islamic state and improving the status of Muslims worldwide. Above all, the Salafi movement is distinguished by its drive to unify Islamic doctrine under its literalist and exclusionary interpretation of Islam, all the while presenting itself as the one true sect, unadulterated by foreign influence and corrupting innovation. This core tendency has defined the activities of Salafis in their relations with other Muslims, including advocating the need for violent resistance.

Muslim activism covers a range of goals and methodology, from educational and cultural missions, to deconstruction of the state in order to create an Islamic state in its stead. The majority of contemporary movements find the existing political and social status of Muslims to be unacceptable, although they differ over the means to rectify this situation and the specific type of action required. Organized Islamic movements hold differing views on a number of key issues pertaining to the role of Muslims in society. These include the legitimate sources of Islamic law, Muslims' relationship to authority and the nature of democracy, the correct means of political involvement and organization, the future direction of the umma, and, of course, the use of violent tactics in bringing about a change in the status of Muslims. Contemporary Salafi activism can essentially be divided into three main categories: reform, or *da'wa* (literally, invitation, proselytizing); political; and jihadi. While these reflect differences in the preferred methodology, a group employs to achieve their aims, the movement as a whole agrees on broad objectives, such as the need for improving the status of Muslims in the West and non-Muslim societies.

Da'wa is an important aspect of all Muslims' faith. For Salafis, however, the purpose of da'wa is less about conversion to Islam per se, than about bringing other Muslims' understanding of Islamic belief and practice in line with their own. While such efforts have been ongoing since the inception of Salafi reformation in eighteenth-century Arabia, today's efforts stem from organizational undertakings by Saudi Salafis beginning in the 1960s. Da'wa activists have promoted *islah* (reform) and *tajdid* (renewal) and generally forbid the use of violent tactics.[9] They reject, however, *ijtihad* (individual interpretation) as a source of law, and decry other Muslims—and other Salafis—who organize for political participation or social activism as partisans undermining Islam. One of the primary aims of these reform-da'wa movements is to "purify" Islam, a process known as *tasfiya*. These movements revolve around scholars who devote their efforts to refuting what they perceive to be erroneous Muslim beliefs and practices that lead the umma astray. The effort of these types of activists has been clearly seen in educational and informational endeavors, especially those in the United States peaking in the 1990s. A number of Muslims influenced by this type of activism have moved on to other forms of activism, with more violent outcomes.

Political Salafi activism is another branch of the movement that has thrived in the United States from the 1960s onward. Political activists such as the Muslim American Society began with close ties to the Muslim Brotherhood platform and organization overseas, but evolved relatively independently in the United States. The activities of large-scale membership organizations like the Muslim Students Association have been aimed at both political activism, social and educational, and da`wa work. Indeed, the lines among the various types of Salafi activism overlap. Yusuf Qaradawi represents one of the most active da`wa-based reformers in the Muslim world, and is one of the best-known clerics in the Muslim world, internationally renowned through satellite television and the Internet. His aims for da`wa activism were elucidated in an Ohio speech in 1995, "Conquest through da`wa, that is what we hope for. . . . We will conquer Europe, we will conquer America, not through the sword but through *da`wa.*"[10]

A set of highly influential militant Salafi clerics reached a large audience through online distribution methods. These contemporary Salafis frequently provide fatwas legitimizing violent acts against unbelievers. Their literature debates the proper meaning and best approach to implementing the Shari`a in the current political climate, rejecting the idea that Muslims can permissibly live under man-made laws. To do so, and willfully participate in a democracy, is depicted as inherently contradictory with the Qur'anic injunctions revealed to humanity, which in their view provide the best legal basis for society. The aim of these scholars and the movement they back is rarely jihad itself. Such Salafi-jihadi scholars seek to persuade Muslims of the need to resist as part of a larger effort to adhere to the practices of the Salaf toward returning to a pure Islamic society, much as reformist and political Salafis do. This movement, however, calls on the individual Muslim to fulfill his or her obligation to Islam through supporting jihad against the "tyrannical" or "oppressive" forces confronting Muslims, prioritizing violent resistance in order to defend the community of believers from outside oppression.

Since the attacks of September 11, there have been hundreds of terrorism-related arrests in the U.S.[11] The following table shows a sample of these arrests, representative of the diverse backgrounds of those involved in terrorism cases. One observes that, based on the arrests, participants or sympathizers of jihad are both converts and Muslims born into the faith. Some were born in the United States, some were naturalized citizens or became legal residents, while a handful were illegal immigrants. The list of arrests includes those of Arab, South Asian, Caribbean, African-American, and European descent.

Name	Age at arrest	Sex	Citizenship	Ethnic/ national background	Conversion to Islam	Plot/group
Shain Duka	26	Male	U.S. resident	Albanian		Ft. Dix group
Eljvir Duka	23	Male	U.S. resident	Albanian		Ft. Dix group
Dritan Duka	28	Male	U.S. resident	Albanian		Ft. Dix group
Mohamad Ibrahim Shnewer	22	Male	U.S.	Palestinian		Ft. Dix group
Agron Abdullahu	24	Male	U.S. resident	Albanian		Ft. Dix group
Serdar Tatar	23	Male	Turkish	Turkish		Ft. Dix group
Habis al-Saoub	38	Male	Jordanian	Palestinian		Portland Seven
Ahmed Bilal	25	Male	U.S.	African-American	Yes	Portland Seven
Muhammad Bilal	22	Male	U.S.	African-American	Yes	Portland Seven
Maher Hawash	39	Male	U.S.	Palestinian		Portland Seven
Patrice Lumumba Ford	33	Male	U.S.	African-American	Yes	Portland Seven
Jeffrey Battle	32	Male	U.S.	African-American		Portland Seven
October Lewis	25	Female	U.S.	African-American		Portland Seven
Yasein Taher	24	Male	U.S.	Yemeni		Lackawanna Six
Mukhtar al-Bakri	22	Male	U.S.	Yemeni		Lackawanna Six
Shafel Mosed	24	Male	U.S.	Yemeni		Lackawanna Six
Faysal Galab	26	Male	U.S.	Yemeni		Lackawanna Six
Sahim Alwan	29	Male	U.S.	Yemeni		Lackawanna Six
Yahya Goba	25	Male	U.S.	Yemeni		Lackawanna Six
Masoud Ahmad Khan	31	Male	U.S.	Pakistani		Virginia Jihad Group

Name	Age at arrest	Sex	Citizenship	Ethnic/ national background	Conversion to Islam	Plot/group
Randall Todd Royer	30	Male	U.S.	Caucasian	Yes	Virginia Jihad Group
Ibrahim Ahmed al-Hamdi	26	Male	Yemeni	Yemeni		Virginia Jihad Group
Yong Ki Kwon	27	Male	U.S.	Korean	Yes	Virginia Jihad Group
Muhammed Aatique	30	Male	Pakistani	Pakistani		Virginia Jihad Group
Seifullah Chapman	30	Male	U.S.	Caucasian	Yes	Virginia Jihad Group
Hammad Abdur-Raheem	35	Male	U.S.	African-American	Yes	Virginia Jihad Group
Donald Surratt	30	Male	U.S.	African-American	Yes	Virginia Jihad Group
Caliph Basha Ibn Abdur-Raheem	29	Male	U.S.	N/A		Virginia Jihad Group
Khwaja Mahmood Hasan	27	Male	U.S.	Pakistani		Virginia Jihad Group
Sabri Benkhala	28	Male	U.S.	Yemeni		Virginia Jihad Group
Ali Asad Chandia	26	Male	Pakistani	Pakistani		Virginia Jihad Group
Ehsanul Islam Sadequee	19	Male	U.S.	Bangladeshi		Atlanta - casing buildings
Syed Haris Ahmed	21	Male	U.S.	Pakistani		Atlanta - casing buildings
Richard C. Reid	28	Male	British	N/A		"Shoe-bomber"
Jose Padilla	31	Male	U.S.	Latino		"Dirty Bomb" plot
Kifah Wael Jayyousi	43	Male	U.S.	Jordanian		"Dirty Bomb" plot
Hamid Hayat	22	Male	U.S.	Pakistani		Lodi, CA
Umer Hayat	47	Male	U.S.	Pakistani		Lodi, CA
Russell Defreitas	63	Male	U.S.	Guyanese		JFK Bomb Plot

Name	Age at arrest	Sex	Citizenship	Ethnic/ national background	Conversion to Islam	Plot/group
Daniel Maldonado	28	Male	U.S.	Puerto Rican	Yes	Support for al-Qa`ida
John Walker Lindh	20	Male	U.S.	Caucasian	Yes	Support for al-Qa`ida
Adam Gadahn	28	Male	U.S.	Caucasian	Yes	Support for al-Qa`ida
Tarik Shah	43	Male	U.S.	African-American		Support for al-Qa`ida
Rafiq Abdus Sabir	52	Male	U.S.	African-American		Support for al-Qa`ida
Abdulrahman Farhane	52	Male	U.S.	Moroccan		Support for al-Qa`ida
Mahmud Faruq Brent	32	Male	U.S.	N/A		Support for al-Qa`ida
Mujahid Abdulqaadir Menepta	51	Male	U.S.	African-American	Yes	Support for al-Qa`ida
Ali al-Tamimi (b. 1963)	40	Male	U.S.	Iraqi		NoVa paintball
Kifah Wael Jayyousi	43	Male	U.S.	Jordanian		Support for al-Qa`ida
Earnest James Ujaama (b. 1966)	36	Male	U.S.	African-American	Yes	Bly, OR - support for al-Qa`ida
Syed Mustajab Shah	54	Male	Pakistani	Pakistani		Drugs for missiles
Muhammed Abid Afridi	29	Male	Pakistani	Pakistani		Drugs for missiles
Ilyas Ali	55	Male	U.S.	Indian		Drugs for missiles
Derrick Shareef	22	Male	U.S.	African-American	Yes	Plot to attack IL mall
Mohammad Ali Hasan Al-Moayad	55	Male	Yemeni	Yemeni		Cleric supporting al-Qa`ida
Mohammed Mohsen Yahya Zayed	29	Male	Yemeni	Yemeni		Asst to al-Moayad
Lyman Faris	33	Male	U.S.	Pakistani		Brooklyn Bridge plot

Name	Age at arrest	Sex	Citizenship	Ethnic/ national background	Conversion to Islam	Plot/group
Nuradin M. Abdi	32	Male	Somali	Somali		Columbus, OH mall plot
Christopher Paul	43	Male	U.S.	African-American	Yes	Columbus, OH mall plot
Haroon Rashid Aswat	26	Male	British	Indian		Bly, OR - support for al-Qa`ida
James Elshafay	19	Male	U.S.	Arab-American		New York subway plot
Shahawar Matin Siraj	23	Male	Pakistani	Pakistani		New York subway plot
Hammad Riaz Samana	21	Male	Pakistani	Pakistani		Los Angeles plots
Kevin James	29	Male	U.S.	African-American	Yes	Los Angeles plots
Levar Washington	25	Male	U.S.	African-American	Yes	Los Angeles plots
Gregory Patterson	21	Male	U.S.	African-American	Yes	Los Angeles plots
Stanley Grant Phanor	31	Male	U.S.	Haitian-American	Yes	Miami group-Sears Tower plot
Patrick Abraham	27	Male	Haitian	Haitian	Yes	Miami group-Sears Tower plot
Narseal Batiste	32	Male	U.S.	Haitian-American	Yes	Miami group-Sears Tower plot
Lyglenson Lemorin	31	Male	U.S.	Haitian	Yes	Miami group-Sears Tower plot
Naudimar Herrera	22	Male	U.S.	Latino	Yes	Miami group-Sears Tower plot
Burson Augustin	21	Male	U.S.	Haitian-American	Yes	Miami group-Sears Tower plot
Rotschild Augustine	22	Male	U.S.	Haitian-American	Yes	Miami group-Sears Tower plot

Sources: U.S. Department of Justice releases; "Terrorist Trial Report Card: U.S. Edition,"
Center on Law and Security, NYU School of Law; Newswire reports.

In early December 2009, five young men from the northern Virginia area were arrested in Pakistan on suspicion of plotting a militant strike. All were U.S. nationals; two were of Pakistani origin, one Egyptian, one Eritrean, and one was Ethiopian. The father of the two Pakistani-Americans (who were brothers) had been initially involved in making connections to the camps for the young men; he himself was a local leader of the Jaish-e-Mohammad militant group.[12] These young men, although lacking in the same level of mentorship, bore many similarities to the Virginia Jihad Group under Ali al-Timimi. The young men were involved with their local branch of ICNA, the Islamic Circle of North America, one of those long-standing activist groups that grew out of the original 1960s MSA organizing efforts.[13]

Those arrests were just part of a very busy year in counterterrorism activities. Over 2009, a number of terrorism arrests made national headlines. They included the uncovering of the Najibullah Zazi case, that of an Afghan native in Colorado charged in September with intending to use weapons of mass destruction. A week later a twenty-one-year-old New York man was charged with conspiring to commit murder abroad for his attempts to join the al-Shabaab militant group in Somalia. The same week, a nineteen-year-old Jordanian man was charged in Texas after attempting to blow up a Dallas building with fake explosives provided by the FBI. That man had been active on jihadi chat rooms, which led the FBI to discover his intentions. Also in late September, FBI agents provided fake explosives to a convert to Islam in Springfield, Illinois, who would attempt to blow up federal buildings in that state's capital. Charged in September, North Carolinian Daniel Patrick Boyd and seven others were arrested in July for plotting to attack the Marine Base at Quantico, about an hour south of Washington, DC. The FBI Academy is located on the base. Boyd had also converted to Islam, and had spent time—like the Virginia Jihad Group—in training camps in Pakistan. Although all of these plots were of differing threat levels and many of the radicalized individuals involved in them were easily detected, the frequency of the incidents show a steady increase. All of these individuals were moved to action by the same group and message—that of militant Salafism and its call to defend the global community of Muslims.

Yet another 2009 plotter, Tarek Mehanna, was indicted in November for providing military support to a terrorist group and conspiring to commit murder. Mehanna, along with his co-conspirators, were plotting to go on a shooting spree in a mall. Such an attack would be easy to carry out and inflict a great amount of terror on the population. Mehanna and an accomplice attempted to get jihadi training at a camp in Yemen in 2004, but returned to the United States unsuccessful. Two years later they tried to join a Lashkar-e-Taiba camp in Pakistan but were again unable to achieve entry. After these failures, they concocted plans of their own to strike at a shopping center. The tactical planning was rather unremarkable, but Mehanna's involvement in Salafi publishing online makes the case worthy of added consideration. The twenty-seven-year-old Massachusetts man, a dual citizen of the United States and Egypt, had at one time tried to establish a media wing for al-Qa'ida in Iraq, and took to distributing messages from its leadership on various online forums.[14] Mehanna was also active in translating Salafi-jihadi texts and publishing and distributing them online. One translation of the well-known "39 Ways to Serve and Participate in Jihad" was posted through At-Tibyan Publishing, a clearinghouse of English-language jihadi texts. Mehanna, like scores of other American Muslims since 9/11, traversed down a path of Salafi activism that led to violent intent.

While some of these cases appear to be individuals—"lone wolves" radicalizing themselves online and acting alone—some were indeed networked. Mehanna had initially been arrested in 2007 for lying to federal investigators about his knowledge of Daniel Maldonado and his jihadi training in Somalia. Mehanna and Maldonado had met at a Massachusetts mosque before the latter had moved to Houston, seeking out an Muslim community that he thought was better suited to his ideals and understanding of Islam. During the first meeting between the two young men, they watched a video of the suffering of Muslims in Bosnia and Palestine; later discussions came to include suicide bombings and the killing of Americans.[15] Once Maldonado had arrived in Somalia, he sent coded communiqués to Mehanna about his training and how he could get into the camps to join him. Mehanna had also been in contact with Daniel Boyd. More than that, he organized a letter-writing campaign for

Ali al-Timimi to protest his imprisonment. Mehanna was not simply a disaffected Muslim obsessing over videos on the Internet; he was part of a militant-leaning Salafi community in America, connected both online and in person.

This trend of Salafi activists turning to militancy seems well set to continue into the future. The current strand of Salafism that espouses jihad as one of its primary tenets can be traced back to the ideologues who rose to prominence in the last three decades, Qutb and ʿAzzam in particular. It is a movement dedicated to political and social change through violent means, attempting to cloak itself in the legitimacy of the Qur'an and teachings of the Prophet. Because of the simplicity of this argument, Salafis have been able to sway great numbers of Muslims across the world and imbue their message into Islamic communities. And Salafi ideology is inextricably connected to violence—"jihadist terrorism," "Islamist militancy,"—whatever it may be called.

Far too often, Salafism is reduced to fundamentalism, people taking their religion too seriously. Salafis are contrasted with "moderate" Muslims with the implication that an overdose of piety is what sets the former apart from the latter. But piety is not the criterion for understanding the place of Salafism within Islam. It is critically important to establish that Islamist violence is not a measure of Muslim piety, or how closely one adheres to Islamic teachings, but rather the acceptance of a set of radical doctrines that grew out of the Salafi movement, itself evolving over the last two centuries. The jihadi trend has been active for more than twenty years, and terrorist acts in the West will not fade away on their own. The Western world must familiarize itself with this ideology, accept the tremendous role it plays in inspiring Islamist violence, and move toward policies and practices that can bring this trend to an end.

Notes

PROLOGUE

1. Timothy Roche and Brian Bennett, et al., "The Making of John Walker Lindh," *Time*, October 7, 2002.
2. Josh Tyrangiel, "The Taliban Next Door," *Time*, December 9, 2001.
3. Roche and Bennett, "The Making of John Walker Lindh."
4. Roche and Bennett, "The Making of John Walker Lindh."
5. See Daniel Benjamin, "The Convert's Zeal: Why Are So Many Jihadists Converts to Islam?," Sept. 7, 2007, http://www.brookings.edu/articles/2007/0907terrorism_benjamin.aspx; and Pew Forum on Religion and Public Life, "The "Zeal of the Convert": Is It the Real Deal?," October 28, 2009, http://pewforum.org/The-Zeal-of-the-Convert-Is-It-the-Real-Deal.aspx.
6. Gregory Johnsen, "Yemen's Al-Iman University: A Pipeline for Fundamentalists?," *Terrorism Monitor* 4 (November 2006): 1–3.
7. This was the position of *Yemen Times* reporter Muhammad bin Salam.
8. Roche and Bennett, "The Making of John Walker Lindh."
9. United States of America v. John Philip Walker Lindh, Grand Jury Indictment, United States District Court, Eastern District of Virginia, February 2002.
10. Prepared Statement of John Walker Lindh to the United States District Court, Eastern District of Virginia, October 4, 2002.

CHAPTER 1. WHAT IS SALAFISM?

1. Ibn Maaja, Kitab al-Fitan, 3986; The Arabic, *al-Tubah li'l-Ghurabaa'*, means the Tree of Paradise, known as al-Tubah, is promised for the Strangers.

2. These deviancies were laid out in Ibn 'Abd al-Wahhab's books *Nawaqidh al-Islam* (Things That Nullify One's Islam) and *al-Qawa'id al-'Arba'a* (Four Principles of Polytheism), among others.

3. Abdulaziz H. Al-Fahad, "From Exclusivism to Accommodation: Doctrinal and Legal Evolution of Wahhabism," *New York University Law Review* 79 (2004): 485.

4. See G.F. Haddad, "Texts By Shaykh Gibril F. Haddad," http://www.abc.se/~m9783/tgfh.html, and Hamid Algar, *Wahhabism: A Critical Essay* (Oneonta, NY: Islamic Publications International, 2002).

5. Shaykh as-Sayyid Yusuf al-Rifa'i, *Nasiha li Ikhwanina 'Ulama' Najd* (Advice to Our Brothers the Scholars of the Najd), http://www.sunnah.org/arabic/mawldhouse/Wahabi_desecration_Sh_Rifai.htm.

6. See "History of the Cemetery of Jannat al-Baqi, http://www.al-islam.org/shrines/baqi.htm.

7. "Who are al-Ghurabaa' (the Strangers)?" October 22, 2005, http://www.islamicthinkers.com/index/index.php?option=com_content&task=view&id=358&Itemid=26.

8. Salafis are greatly inspired by the concept of the Saved Sect (*al-firqa al-najiyya*) and the related concept of the victorious sect (*al-ta'ifa al-mansura*). This is rooted in the hadith: "The Prophet said, 'The Jews split into 71 sects: one will enter Paradise and 70 will enter Hell. The Christians split into 72 sects: 71 will enter Hell and one will enter Paradise. By Him in Whose hand is my soul, my Ummah will split into 73 sects: one will enter Paradise and 72 will enter Hell.' Someone asked, 'O Messenger of Allah, who will they be?' He replied, 'The main body of the Muslims (al-Jama'ah)'" (hadith reported by Awf ibn Malik). The version taken to heart by the Salafis adds: "The Prophet goes onto say that the saved sect, 'Are those who follow my and my companion's path'" (Sunan al-Tirmidhi).

9. See biography from efatwa.com (or mirror fatwa-online.com), a site that promotes the fatwas and press releases of Bin Baz and other members of the Permanent Committee.

10. Albert Hourani, *Arabic Thought in the Liberal Age 1798–1939* (Cambridge: Cambridge University Press, 1962), 109.

11. Hourani, *Arabic Thought,* 109–112.

CHAPTER 2. SALAFISM AND THE REDEFINITION OF MUSLIM IDENTITY

1. From "Answer of Jamal al-Din to Renan," *Journal des Débats,* 18 May 1883, in Nikki R. Keddie, *An Islamic Response to Imperialism: Political*

and Religious Writings of Sayyid Jamal al-Din "al-Afghani" (Berkeley: University of California Press, 1983), 183.

2. See Nadav Safran, *Saudi Arabia: The Ceaseless Quest for Security* (Ithaca, NY: Cornell University Press, 1988).

3. Albert Hourani, *Arabic Thought in the Liberal Age* (Cambridge: Cambridge University Press, 1962), 114.

4. Rashid Rida, in *al-Manar* 24: 311.

5. Sayyid Jamal al-Din Muhammad b. Safdar al-Afghani (1838–1897), Center for Islam and Science (CIS), available at: http://www.cis-ca.org/voices/a/afghni.htm.

6. Christopher Henzel, "The Origins of al Qaeda's Ideology: Implications for U.S. Strategy," *Parameters* 35 (January 2005), 71.

7. Hourani, *Arabic Thought,* 131–32.

8. Henzel, "The Origins of al Qaeda's Ideology," 72–73.

9. Hourani, *Arabic Thought,* 134.

10. Ibid., 139.

11. David Commins, *The Wahhabi Mission and Saudi Arabia* (London and New York: I.B. Tauris, 2006), 132.

12. Safran, *Saudi Arabia,* 19.

13. Ibid., 32.

14. Safran, *Saudi Arabia,* 37.

15. See Gerald De Gaury, *The Rulers of Mecca* (New York: Dorset Press, 1991).

16. Dayan Kostiner, et al., *The Making of Saudi Arabia, 1916–1936: From Chieftaincy to Monarchical State* (London: Oxford University Press, 1993), 53.

17. See Malcolm H. Kerr, *Islamic Reform: The Political and Legal Theories of Muhammad `Abduh and Rashid Rida* (Berkeley and Los Angeles: University of California Press, 1966).

18. Ahmad al-Sharabasi, *Rashid Rida Sahib al-Manar* [Rashid Rida the Founder of al-Manar] (Cairo: Matabi' al-Ahram at-Tijariyyah, 1970).

19. Hourani, *Arabic Thought,* 224–26.

20. Rashid Rida, "Tarikh al-ustadh al-imam al-Shaykh Muhammad `Abduh" [The History of Shaykh and Teacher Muhammad `Abduh], 303; cited in Hourani, *Arabic Thought,* 226.

21. Commins, *The Wahhabi Mission,* 138.

22. See Richard Mitchell, *The Society of Muslim Brothers* (New York: Oxford University Press, 1993), and Brynjar Lia, *The Society of the Muslim Brothers in Egypt: The Rise of an Islamic Mass Movement* (Reading, UK: Ithaca Press, 1998).

23. Ziad Munsen, "Islamic Mobilization: Social Movement Theory and the Muslim Brotherhood," *Sociological Quarterly* 42, no. 44 (2002): 489.

24. Munsen, "Islamic Mobilization," 490.

25. Ibid.

26. Munsen, "Islamic Mobilization," 491.

27. Mitchell, *Society of Muslim Brothers.*

28. Gilles Kepel, *Muslim Extremism in Egypt: The Pharoah and the Prophet* (Berkeley and Los Angeles: University of California Press, 1984), 37.

29. Lawrence Davidson, *Islamic Fundamentalism: An Introduction* (Westport, CT: Greenwood Press, 2003), 86.

30. From the now defunct Salaf Misr [Salaf Egypt] online forum, http://www. salafmisr.com/vb/showthread.php?t=2547.

31. Peter Bergen, *Holy War, Inc: Inside the Secret World of Osama bin Laden.* (London: Orion Books, 2002).

32. U.S. Special Operations Command (SOCOM) Harmony Document 2RAD-2004–600457, February 14, 2006.

CHAPTER 3. IDEAS TRANSFORMED INTO ACTION

1. Lawrence Wright, *The Looming Tower: Al-Qaeda and the Road to 9/11* (New York: Knopf, 2006), 36.

2. *Militant Ideology Atlas*, Combating Terrorism Center at the United States Military Academy, 2005, available at: http://ctc.usma.edu/atlas.

3. Wright, *Looming Tower,* 22–28.

4. Sayyid Qutb, *Milestones,* available at: http://www.youngmuslims.ca.

5. Published in the CTC's *Militant Ideology Atlas,* on which the author worked.

6. Oxford Dictionary of Islam, "Qutb, Muhammad," Oxford Islamic Studies Online, http://www.oxfordislamicstudies.com/article/opr/t125/e1954?_hi=3&_pos=22.

7. See Gilles Kepel, *Jihad: The Trail of Political Islam* (London: I. B. Tauris, 2006).

8. Gilles Kepel. *Muslim Extremism in Egypt: The Prophet and the Pharaoh* (Berkeley: University of California Press, 1985), 61–62.

9. Kepel, *Muslim Extremism in Egypt,* 64.

10. Wright, *Looming Tower,* 91.

11. Sayyid Qutb quoted in John L. Esposito, *Unholy War: Terror in the Name of Islam* (New York: Oxford University Press, 2002), 60.

12. *CTC Militant Ideology Atlas.*

13. Youssef Aboul-Enein, "Sheikh Abdel-Fatah Al-Khalidi Revitalizes Sayid Qutb: Inside the Adversary's Anti-American Ideology from the Cold

War to Operation Iraqi Freedom," Combating Terrorism Center, United States Military Academy, http://ctc.usma.edu.

14. "Founder: Syed Moudoodi biography at a glance," Jamaat-i-Islami Karachi branch website, http://www.karachijamaat.org/webpages/Founder.asp

15. *CTC Militant Ideology Atlas.*

16. "Founder: Syed Moudoodi biography at a glance," Jamaat-i-Islami Karachi branch website, available at: http://www.karachijamaat.org/webpages/Founder.asp

17. Mas'ud ibn Zahur ibn Hamid'ullah Ahmed Khan al-Jarral al-Hanafi, "Abu'l 'Ala Maududi's Calumniations against the Great Prophets and Companions of the Ummah," http://www.sunnah.org; and author interview with Mahan Abedin in the U.K. by phone, June 1, 2008.

18. Wright, *Looming Tower,* 105–7.

19. "Mawdudi, Qutb and the Prophets of Allaah," Salafi Publications, http://www.salafipublications.com/sps/sp.cfm?subsecID=NDV08&articleID=NDV080001&articlePages=1.

20. Ibid.

21. Noreen Ahmed-Ullah, Sam Roe, and Laurie Cohen, "A Rare Look at Secretive Brotherhood in America," *Chicago Tribune,* September 19, 2004.

22. Larry Poston, *Islamic Da`wah in the West: Muslim Missionary Activity and the Dynamics of Conversion to Islam* (Oxford: Oxford University Press, 1992), 79.

23. Ahmed-Ullah, Roe, and Cohen, "A Rare Look at Secretive Brotherhood in America."

24. "The North American Islamic Trust—NAIT," http://www.nait.net.

25. See "American Muslims' Campaign against Egypt's HR Abuses Heats Up," Ikhwanweb.info; see also http://masnet.org.

26. Ahmed-Ullah, Roe, and Cohen. "A Rare Look at Secretive Brotherhood in America."

27. Brendan Lyons, "Religious leader tied to terror," *Times Union,* June 30, 2002.

28. "About MAS," Muslim American Society, http://masnet.org/aboutmas.asp.

29. The website's URL is: http://www.whyislam.org; it also operates a corresponding (877) WHY-ISLAM hotline.

30. A list of recommended books listed on the Young Muslims website, http://www.ymsite.com/books.php?new_template=yes.

CHAPTER 4. THE TRIUMPH OF ISLAM OVER GODLESSNESS

1. The *Kata'ib Shuhada `Abdullah `Azzam* (The Martyr `Abdullah `Azzam Brigades) are just one blatant example of `Azzam's legacy. The group,

which has also called itself al-Qa'ida in Syria and Egypt, claimed responsibility for the October 2004 attacks (along with other groups) at the Sinai tourist resorts of Taba and Ras Shitan that killed thirty-four people. The Brigades posted a claim of responsibility on an Islamist web forum, stating that the attacks were in response to the "crimes of worldwide evil powers" in Iraq, Afghanistan, Palestine, and Chechnya.

2. Andrew McGregor, "Jihad and the Rifle Alone: `Abdullah `Azzam and the Islamist Revolution," *Journal of Conflict Studies* 23 (Fall 2003).

3. Trevor Stanley, "Abdullah `Azzam, 'The Godfather of Jihad,'" Perspectives on World History and Current Events Middle East Project, http://www.pwhce.org/azzam.html.

4. "Profiles of Ash Shuhadaa," Ummah Forum, http://www.ummah.com/forum/showthread.php?t=5062.

5. Peter Bergen, *Holy War, Inc: Inside the Secret World of Osama bin Laden* (London: Orion Books, 2002).

6. "Profiles of Ash Shuhadaa," http://www.ummah.com/forum/showthread.php?t=5062.

7. McGregor, "Jihad and the Rifle Alone."

8. From "`Abdullah `Azzam, Miraculous Signs of Allah the Compassionate regarding the Afghans' Jihad (*Ayat al-rahman fi jihad al-Afghan*)," *CTC Militant Ideology Atlas* (1984), 37–39.

9. Abdullah `Azzam, Miraculous Signs of Allah the Compassionate, *CTC Militant Ideology Atlas*, 37–39.

10. Benjamin Weiser, Susan Sachs, and David Kocieniewski, "U.S. Sees Brooklyn Link to World Terror Network," *New York Times,* October 22, 1998.

11. Robert Friedman, "The CIA's Jihad," *The New Yorker,* March 1995.

12. Friedman, "The CIA's Jihad."

13. Islamic Society of North America letter from August 8, 1991, soliciting donations for al-Kifah Refugee Center, http://www.investigativeproject.org/documents/misc/8.pdf.

14. Andrew Marshall, "Terror 'Blowback' Burns CIA," *The Independent,* November 1, 1998.

15. See United States District Court, District of Massachusetts, United States v. Muhamed Mubayyid and Emaddin Z. Muntasser, Grand Jury Indictment.

16. See *CTC Militant Ideology Atlas*.

17. Al-Maqdisi interview with the now-defunct *Nida' al-Islam* magazine, 1997.

18. Nibras Kazimi, "A Virulent Ideology in Mutation: Zarqawi Upstages Maqdisi," *Current Trends in Islamist Ideology* 2 (September 2005).

19. Abu Muhammad al-Maqdisi, *Hiwar ma' al-shaykh Abi Muhammad al-Maqdisi* (An Interview with Shaykh Abu Muhammad al-Maqdisi), 2002, http://tawhed.ws.

20. Abu Muhammad al-Maqdisi, *Hadhihi 'aqidatuna* (This is Our Doctrine), 2003.

21. Abu Muhammad al-Maqdisi, *al-Kawashif al-jaliyya fi kufr al-dawla al-Sa`udiyya* (The Shameful Actions Manifest in the Saudi State's Disbelief), 2000.

22. Al-Maqdisi, *al-Kawashif al-jaliyya.*

23. Kazimi, "Virulent Ideology in Mutation."

24. Abu Muhammad al-Maqdisi, *Kashf al-niqab 'an Shari`at al-ghab* (Unveiling the Law of the Jungle), 1988, http://tawhed.ws.

25. Al-Maqdisi, *al-Kawashif al-jaliyya.*, 227.

CHAPTER 5. COVERT ORGANIZING

1. *Le Nouvel Observateur,* Paris, 15–21 January 1998, http://www.globalresearch.ca/articles/BRZ110A.html.

2. United States Department of the Treasury, Press Release designated BIF a financier of terrorism, pursuant to Executive Order 13224, November 19, 2002.

3. Sam Roe, Laurie Cohen, and Stephen Franklin, "How Saudi Wealth Fueled Holy War," *Chicago Tribune,* February 22, 2004.

4. "U.S. Treasury Designates Two Individuals with Ties to al Qaida, UBL: Former BIF Leader and al-Qaida Associate Named Under E.O. 13224," U.S. Treasury Department Press Release JS-2164, December 21, 2004, http://www.ustreas.gov/press/releases/js2164.htm.

5. Roe, et al., "How Saudi Wealth Fueled Holy War."

6. Ibid.

7. Ibid.

8. Ibid.

9. Ibid.

10. See Indictment, United States v. Enaam Arnaout, United States District Court, Northern District of Illinois, Eastern Division, April 2002.

11. 9–11 Commission Report, National Commission on Terrorist Attacks upon the United States, p. 467, http://www.9–11commission.gov/report/index.htm.

12. "The List of Individuals Belonging to or Associated with the Taliban," The United Nations Al-Qa`ida and Taliban Sanctions Committee, 267, http://www.un.org/sc/committees/1267/consoltablelist.shtml.

13. Roe, et al., "How Saudi Wealth Fueled Holy War."

14. Indictment, U.S. v. Enaam Arnaout.

15. Ibid.

16. Ibid.

17. Ibid.

18. U.S. Department of the Treasury, Press Release designated BIF a financier of terrorism.

19. Indictment, U.S. v. Enaam Arnaout.

20. Indictment, United States v. Masoud Khan et al., United States District Court, Eastern District of Virginia, June 2003.

21. "Wanted: Fazul Abdullah Mohammed," FBI Rewards for Justice, http://www.rewardsforjustice.net/english/index.cfm?page=Fazul.

22. "On the Trail of Man Wanted for Bomb Blast," *The Nation* (Nairobi), May 13, 2006.

23. Phil Hirschkorn, "Elusive Al Qaeda Operative was 'Real Deal,'" *CBS News*, January 10, 2007, http://www.cbsnews.com/.

24. Donald G. McNeil, Jr., "Assets of a Bombing Suspect: Keen Wit, Religious Soul, Angry Temper," *New York Times*, October 6, 1998.

25. Karl Vick, "FBI Trails Embassy Bombing Suspect," *Washington Post*, September 17, 1998.

26. Pérouse de Montclos, Marc-Antoine, Profile of the al-Haramayn Foundation, Observatoire de l'action humanitaire, 2005, http://www.observatoire-humanitaire.org/fusion.php?l=FR&id=73.

27. "On the Trail of Man Wanted for Bomb Blast."

28. Abdullah Muhammad Fazul, Letter to Omar Muhammed Fazul, n.d., http://www.pbs.org/wgbh/pages/frontline/shows/saudi/fazul/letter.html, accessed February 13, 2007.

29. U.S. v. Usama Bin Laden et al., S(9) 98 Cr. 1023, Indictment, pp. 16f.

30. *Anatomy of a Terrorist Attack: An In-Depth Investigation into the 1998 Bombings of the U.S. Embassies in Kenya and Tanzania*, Matthew B. Ridgway Center for Security Studies, University of Pittsburgh, 2005.

31. International Crisis Group, "Counter-terrorism in Somalia," 7.

32. Oriana Zill, A Portrait of Wadih El-Hage, Accused Terrorist, http://www.pbs.org.frontline.

33. Oriana Zill, A Portrait of Wadih El-Hage.

34. Chris Limberis, "Terrorists in Tiny Town," *Tucson Weekly*, September 20, 2001.

35. See Douglas Farah, *Blood From Stones: The Secret Financial Network of Terror* (New York: Broadway Books, 2004).

36. "Bush should heed Hempstone's advice," *The Nation* (Nairobi), September 30, 2005.

37. Abdulsamad Ali, "Kenya: Computer May Hold Clue on Terror Suspect," *The Nation* (Nairobi), January 24, 2007.

38. Olivier Roy, *Globalized Islam: The Search for a New Ummah* (New York: Columbia University Press), 2004, 304–8.

CHAPTER 6. THE FLOW OF SAUDI DOLLARS

1. Quoted in Muhammad ibn Ahmad al-Salim's "39 Ways to Serve and Participate in Jihad," translated by al-Tibyan Publications.

2. Robert Dreyfuss, *Devil's Game: How the United States Helped Unleash Fundamentalist Islam* (New York: Macmillan, 2005), 127–28.

3. Dreyfuss, *Devil's Game,* 128–29.

4. Ibid.

5. Ibid., 131.

6. Gilles Kepel, "The Brotherhood in the Salafist Universe," *Current Trends in Islamist Ideology* 6, (February 2008), 20–28.

7. Translation from audiotape entitled *Sina'at Al-Mawt,* distributed online by the now-defunct `Azzam Publications.

8. See "Callers & Individuals: An Analysis of the Thought and Methodology of Contemporary Individuals," Salafi Publications, http://www.salafipublications.com/sps/sp.cfm?secID=NDV&loadpage=displaysection.cfm.

9. See biography from efatwa.com, a site that promotes the fatwas and press releases of Bin Baz and other members of the Permanent Committee.

10. See http://www.binbaz.org.sa.

11. "Mujahid Usamah Bin Ladin Talks Exclusively to 'NIDA'UL ISLAM' about the New Powder Keg in the Middle East," published in the November 1996 issue of the now-defunct *Nida' al-Islam* (http://www.islam.org.au), http://fas.org/irp/world/para/docs/LADIN.htm.

12. *Ain-Al-Yaqeen* (Saudi newspaper), December 8, 2000.

13. David E. Kaplan, "The Saudi Connection," *U.S. News & World Report,* December 7, 2003.

14. Kaplan, "The Saudi Connection."

15. Ibid.

16. Judith Miller, "The Money Trail: Raids seek evidence of money-laundering," New York Times, March 21, 2002.

17. "Additional Background Information on Charities Designated under Executive Order 13224," United States Department of Treasury, http://www.treas.gov/offices/enforcement/key-issues/protecting/charities_execorder_13224-i.shtml.

18. United States v. Soliman S. Bihieri, Declaration in Support of Pre-Trial Detention, United States District Court, Eastern District of Virginia, August 14, 2003.

19. Glenn R. Simpson, "The U.S. Provides Details of Terror-Financing Web," *Wall Street Journal,* September 15, 2003.

20. In the Matter of Searches Involving 555 Grove Street, Herndon, Virginia, and Related Locations, (Redacted) Affidavit in Support of Application for Search Warrant, United States District Court for the Eastern District of Virginia, October 2003.

21. In the Matter of Searches Involving 555 Grove Street.

22. Simpson, "Funds under Terror Probe Flowed from Offshore."

23. John Mintz and Tom Jackman, "Finances Prompted Raids on Muslims: U.S. suspected terrorism ties to N.Va. for years," *Washington Post,* March 24, 2002.

24. Operation Green Quest Overview, February 26, 2002, http://www.cbp.gov/ xp/cgov/newsroom/news_releases/archives/legacy/2002/22002/ 02262002.xml.

25. In the Matter of Searches Involving 555 Grove Street.

26. Mintz and Jackman, "Finances Prompted Raids on Muslims."

27. From the organization's website, http://www.iiit.org.

28. United States v. Holy Land Relief Foundation, et al. Government exhibit 003–0003.

29. Zeyno Baran, "The Muslim Brotherhood's U.S. Network," *Current Trends in Islamist Ideology* 6, (February 27, 2008).

30. "ISNA Recognizes IIIT VP Dr. Jamal Barzinji for Pioneering Service," International Institute of Islamic Thought, September 8, 2008, available at: http://www.iiit.org/NewsEvents/News/tabid/62/articleType/Article View/articleId/90/Default.aspx.

31. Simpson, *"Funds under Terror Probe Flowed from Offshore."*

32. Greg Palast and David Pallister, "FBI claims Bin Laden inquiry was frustrated," *Guardian*, November 7, 2001.

33. Palast and Pallister, "FBI claims Bin Laden inquiry was frustrated."

34. See U.S. v. Enaam Arnaout.

35. Ahmad Totonji, "Muslims in the Caribbean: Towards Increased Cooperation and Integration," August 26, 2009, http://ahmadtotonji.net/index. php?option=com_content&view=article&id=10:muslims-in-the-caribbe- an-towards-increased-co-operation-and-integration&catid=19:biography &Itemid=31.

36. Biography of Dr. Taha Jabir al-Alwani, Center for the Study of Islam and

Democracy, available at: https://www.csidonline.org/about-csid/board-of-directors/past-directors/116-former-directors/24-taha-jaber-al-alawani.

37. "History of the Fiqh Council," The Fiqh Council of North America, http://www.fiqhcouncil.org/AboutUs/tabid/175/Default.aspx.

38. "Taha Jabir Alalwani," Graduate School of Islamic and Social Sciences, available at: http://www.cordobauniversity.org/gsiss/faculty/Alalwani.asp.

39. Tom Jackman, "N.Va. Sites Raided in Probe of Terrorism: Federal agencies seek information on funds," *Washington Post,* March 21, 2002, and Mintz and Jackman, "Finances Prompted Raids on Muslims."

40. Susan Schmidt, "September 11 Families Join to Sue Saudis: Banks, charities and royals accused of funding al Qaeda terrorist network," The *Washington Post*, August 16, 2002.

41. Chris Mondics, "Cozen O'Connor dealt blow in 9/11 lawsuit," *Philadelphia Inquirer,* August 15, 2008.

CHAPTER 7. SALAFI INFLUENCE IN AMERICA

1. From "Say No to Oppression," circulated by At-Tibyan Publications on Internet forums.

2. "Muzammil Siddiqi, Past President," ISNA, http://www.isna.net/ISNAHQ/pages/Muzammil-Siddiqi.aspx.

3. Various population figures include 2.5 million by the Pew Research Center: Tracy Miller, ed. (October 2009), *Mapping the Global Muslim Population: A Report on the Size and Distribution of the World's Muslim Population*, Pew Research Center, http://pewforum.org/newassets/images/reports/Muslimpopulation/Muslimpopulation.pdf.

4. From the U.S. State Department and Pew Forum on Religion and Public Life.

5. "Salafi Directory of North America," Salafi Talk Discussion Forum, available at: http://www.salafitalk.net/st/printthread.cfm?Forum=19&Topic=4923.

6. The Al-Quraan wa As-Sunnah Society of New York, http://www.albaseerah.org.

7. September 11 Web Archive Collection, Library of Congress (archived: November 4, 2001), http://webarchives.loc.gov/collections/lcwa0001/20011102201206/http://www.iiasa.org/.

8. Ibid.

9. Ibid.

10. Ibid.

11. Caryle Murphy and Susan Schmidt, "U.S. Revokes Visas of 16 at Islamic Institute," *Washington Post,* January 29, 2004.

12. Jerry Markon and Susan Schmidt, "Islamic Institute raided in Fairfax," *Washington Post*, July 2, 2004.

13. "Feds raid Saudi-based institute in Fairfax," Associated Press, July 1, 2004.

14. "Islamic institute closed, searched," *Washington Times*, July 1, 2004.

15. Biography of Jaafar Idris, http://www.jaafaridris.com/English/Biography .htm.

16. Jacqui Salmon and Joe Holley, "Federal Agency Recommends Closing Saudi School in Va.," *Washington Post,* October 18, 2007.

17. Salmon and Holley, "Federal Agency Recommends Closing Saudi School in Va."

18. "About ISA," The Islamic Saudi Academy of Washington, available at: http://www.saudiacademy.net/2008AboutISA.html.

19. Susan Schmidt, "Spreading Saudi Fundamentalism in U.S.," *Washington Post*, October 2, 2003.

20. Paul M. Barrett and Glenn R. Simpson, "Prominent Saudi Draws U.S. Focus," *Wall Street Journal,* October 2, 2003.

21. Schmidt, "Spreading Saudi Fundamentalism in U.S."

22. Ibid.

23. "Muslims inmates [sic]," Islamic Assembly of North America, available at: http://www.iananet.org/inmate.htm.

24. Schmidt, "Spreading Saudi Fundamentalism in U.S."

25. "Magazine writers moved on to Islamist groups," *Pittsburgh Tribune-Review*, August 4, 2002.

26. "About IANA," Islamic Assembly of North America, available at: http://www.iananet.org/about.htm#Activities.

27. Ibid.

28. Ibid.

29. "Magazine writers moved on to Islamist groups," *Pittsburgh Tribune-Review*.

30. Ibid.

31. Second Superseding Indictment, United States v. Sami Omar alHussayen, United States District Court for the District of Idaho.

32. "Magazine writers moved on to Islamist groups," *Pittsburgh Tribune-Review*.

33. Schmidt, "Spreading Saudi Fundamentalism in U.S."

34. Umar Lee, "The Rise and Fall of the Salafi Dawah in the United States," originally posted on http://umarlee.com/ in January 2007, full version archived at: http://www.archive.org/details/TheRiseAndFallOfTheSalafi-DawahInTheUnitedStates.

35. Umar Lee, "The Rise and Fall of the Salafi Dawah in the United States."

CHAPTER 8. ANATOMY OF A TERRORISM CASE

1. Mary Beth Sheridan, "Hardball Tactics in an Era of Threats," *Washington Post*, September 3, 2006.

2. United States of America v. Ali al-Timimi, Indictment, in United States District Court, Eastern District of Virginia.

3. Sheridan, "Hardball Tactics in an Era of Threats."

4. See United States v. Masoud Khan et al., Court Memorandum Opinion, United States District Court for the Eastern District of Virginia, March 4, 2004.

5. Indictment, United States of America v. Ali al-Timimi.

6. Mitchell Silber and Arvin Bhatt, "Radicalization in the West: The Homegrown Threat," New York Police Department, 60.

7. Jerry Markon, "Final 'Va. Jihad' Defendant Acquitted," *Washington Post*, March 10, 2004.

8. Milton Viorst, "The Education of Ali al-Timimi," *Atlantic Monthly*, http://www.islamicawakening.com/viewnews.php?newsID=4139.

9. "Ali Al-Timimi: A Life of Learning," Islamic Awakening, March 24, 2005, http://www.islamicawakening.com/viewnews.php?newsID=4139.

10. Ibid.

11. Viorst, "The Education of Ali al-Timimi."

12. Ibid.

13. Umar Lee, "The Rise and Fall of the Salafi Dawah in the United States," originally posted on http://umarlee.com/ in January 2007, full version archived at: http://www.archive.org/details/TheRiseAndFallOfTheSalafi-DawahInTheUnitedStates.

14. U.S. v. Masoud Khan, et al., Court Memorandum Opinion, 17.

15. "Prisoners: U.S.: Hammad Abdurraheem," Cage Prisoners profile of Hammad Abdur-Raheem, available at: http://www.cageprisoners.com/prisoners.php?id=1348.

16. U.S. v. Masoud Khan, et al., Court Memorandum Opinion, 45.

17. Stephen Baxter, "Hanover a stop in jihadist's travels," *York Daily Register*, November 21, 2004.

18. Baxter, "Hanover a stop in jihadist's travels."

19. U.S. v. Masoud Khan, et al., Court Memorandum Opinion, 17.

20. United States v. Randall Todd Royer, et al. Indictment, United States District Court, Eastern District of Virginia, June, 2003.

21. "Guest CV: Nihad Awad, Ismael Royer," http://www.islamonline.net/live dialogue/english/Guestcv.asp?hGuestID=605R88.

22. "Randall Todd Royer and Ibrahim al-Hamdi Sentenced for Participation

in Virginia Jihad Network,"U.S. Department of Justice Press Release, April 9, 2004, http://www.justice.gov/opa/pr/2004/April/04_crm_225.htm.

23. Silber and Bhatt, "Radicalization in the West," 61.
24. U.S. v. Ali al-Timimi, Government exhibit 7, A3.
25. U.S. v. Ali al-Timimi, Charging Affadavit, Statement of Ibrahim al-Hamdi.
26. Ibid.
27. Ibid.
28. Ibid.
29. Ibid.
30. United States v. Ali al-Timimi, Indictment.
31. Ibid.
32. U.S. v. Masoud Khan, et al., Court Memorandum Opinion, 48.
33. Ibid., 48–49.
34. Ibid.
35. U.S. v. Randall Todd Royer, et al., Indictment.

CHAPTER 9. RADICALIZATION

1. *Militant Ideology Atlas*, Top 20 Texts, http://ctc.usma.edu/atlas.
2. Criminal complaint, United States v. Shain Duka et al. United States District Court, District of New Jersey, filed May 7, 2007.
3. Stephen Ulph. "A Guide to Jihad on the Web," *Terrorism Focus* 2 (March 31, 2005), http://www.jamestown.org/programs/gta/single/?tx_ttnews[tt_news]=169&tx_ttnews[backPid]=238&no_cache=1.
4. Chris Heffelfinger, "Online Jihadi Forums Provide Curriculum for Aspiring Mujahideen," *Terrorism Focus* 3 (October 24, 2006), http://www.jamestown.org/programs/gta/single/?tx_ttnews[tt_news]=946&tx_ttnews[backPid]=239&no_cache=1.
5. "Chronology: The Lackawanna Investigation," PBS Frontline, http://www.pbs.org/wgbh/pages/frontline/shows/sleeper/inside/cron.html.
6. Testimony of John S. Pistole, Assistant Director, Counterterrorism Division, FBI, before the Senate Judiciary Committee, Subcommittee on Terrorism, Technology, and Homeland Security, October 14, 2003.
7. See "A Review of the Bureau of Prisons' Selection of Muslim Religious Services Providers," April 2004, Office of the Inspector General, U.S. Department of Justice.
8. Frequently spelled Jam'iyyat Ul-Islam Is-Saheeh or Jamaat Ul Islam As Saheeh.
9. Timothy Roche, et al. "The Making of John Walker Lindh," *Time*, October 7, 2002.
10. U.S. Department of Justice Press Release #07-531, "U.S. Citizen Sen-

tenced to Prison for Receiving Military Training from a Terrorist Organization," July 20, 2007.

11. Posting on Islamicnetworking.com, in reply to "Cleric who urged jihad to be freed," August 22, 2006 (accessed on November 12, 2007).

12. Criminal Complaint against Daniel Maldonado in United States District Court, Southern District of Texas, February 13, 2007.

CHAPTER 10. THE TREND CONTINUES

1. BBC News, "Profile: Anwar al-Awlaki," January 3, 2010, http://news.bbc.co.uk/go/pr/fr/-/2/hi/middle_east/8438635.stm.

2. Susan Schmidt, "Imam from Va. Mosque Now Thought to Have Aided Al-Qaeda," *Washington Post*, February 27, 2008.

3. Schmidt, "Imam From Va. Mosque Now Thought to Have Aided Al-Qaeda."

4. Brian Handwerk and Zain Habboo, "Attack on America: An Islamic Scholar's Perspective—Part 1, *National Geographic News,* September 28, 2001, http://news.nationalgeographic.com/news/2001/09/0927_imam part1 .html.

5. Schmidt, "Imam from Va. Mosque Now Thought to Have Aided Al-Qaeda."

6. Ibid.

7. Scott Shane, "Born in U.S., a Radical Cleric Inspires Terror," *New York Times*, November 18, 2009.

8. Andrea Elliot, "A Call to Jihad, Answered in America," *New York Times*, July 12, 2009.

9. Quintan Wiktorowicz, *The Management of Islamic Activism: Salafis, the Muslim Brotherhood, and State Power in Jordan* (Albany: State University of New York, 2001), 113–14.

10. John Mintz and Douglas Farah, "In Search of Friends among The Foes," *Washington Post*, September 11, 2004.

11. U.S. Department of Justice, Office of the Inspector General, "The Department of Justice's Internal Controls over Terrorism Reporting," http://www.usdoj.gov/oig/reports/plus/a0720/final.pdf.

12. "FBI Questions U.S. Nationals Held over Al-Qa`idah Links," AFP news agency, December 10, 2009.

13. Scott Shane, "Pakistan Detains Five Americans in Raid Tied to Militants," *New York Times*, December 9, 2009.

14. See United States v. Tarek Mehanna, Criminal Complaint, filed in United States District Court, Eastern District of Massachusetts.

15. United States v. Tarek Mehanna, Criminal Complaint.

Selected Bibliography

Abdo, Geneive. *No God but God: Egypt and the Triumph of Islam*. Oxford: Oxford University Press, 2000.

'Abduh, Muhammad. *Risalat al-Tawhid [Letters on Monotheism]*. Cairo, 1942.

AbuKhalil, As'ad. *Bin Laden, Islam and America's New "War on Terrorism."* New York: Seven Stories Press, 2002.

Al al-Shaykh, 'Abd al-Rahman ibn 'Abd al-Latif. *Mashahir 'ulama' najd wa ghayruhum [Famous Scholars of the Najd and Elsewhere]*. Saudi Arabia, 1974.

———. *'Ulama' al-Da'wa [Scholars of Proselytization]* Saudi Arabia, 1966.

Algar, Hamid. *Wahhabism: A Critical Essay*. New York: Islamic Publications International, 2002.

Scheuer, Michael (as Anonymous). *Through Our Enemies' Eyes: Osama Bin Laden, Radical Islam & the Future of America*. Washington, DC: Brasseys, 2002.

Arkoun, Mohammed. *Islam: To Reform or to Subvert*. London: Saqi Books, 2006.

———. *Al-Islam: Naqd wa'ijtihad [Criticism and Consensus]*. Beirut: Dar al-Saqi, 1990.

———. *The Unthought in Contemporary Islamic Thought*. London: Saqi Books, 2002.

Atwan, Abdel Bari. *The Secret History of al-Qaida*. London: Abacus, 2006.

Barrett, Paul M. *American Islam: The Struggle for the Soul of a Religion*. New York: Farrar, Straus and Giroux, 2007.

Benjamin, Daniel and Steven Simon. *The Age of Sacred Terror*. New York: Random House, 2003.

Bergen, Peter. *Holy War, Inc.: Inside the Secret World of Osama bin Laden.* New York: Free Press, 2001.

Bradley, John R. *Saudi Arabia Exposed.* New York: Palgrave Macmillan, 2005.

Burgat, Francois. *Face to Face with Political Islam.* London and New York: I.B. Tauris, 2003.

Burke, Jason. *Al-Qaida: Casting a Shadow of Terror.* London and New York: I.B. Tauris, 2003.

Coll, Steve. *The Bin Ladens: An Arabian Family in the American Century.* New York: Penguin Press, 2008.

Commins, David. *The Wahhabi Mission and Saudi Arabia.* London and New York: I. B. Tauris, 2006.

De Gaury, Gerald. *The Rulers of Mecca.* New York: Dorset Press, 1991.

Dreyfuss, Robert. *Devil's Game: How the United States Helped Unleash Fundamentalist Islam.* New York: Macmillan, 2005.

Esposito, John L. *Unholy War: Terror in the Name of Islam.* New York: Oxford University Press, 2002.

Fandy, Mamoun. *Saudi Arabia and the Politics of Dissent.* New York: Palgrave Macmillan, 1999.

Fahad(al-), Abdulaziz H. "Commentary: From Exclusivism to Accommodation: Doctrinal and Legal Evolution of Wahhabism." *New York University Law Review* 2, (2004): 485–519.

Fuller, Graham E. *The Future of Political Islam.* New York: Palgrave Macmillan, 2003.

Haykel, Bernard. *Revival and Reform in Islam: The Legacy of Muhammad al-Shawkani.* Cambridge: Cambridge University Press, 2003.

Hourani, Albert. *Arabic Thought in the Liberal Age 1798–1939.* Cambridge: Cambridge University Press, 1962.

Hudaybi(al-), Hasan. *Du`a la quda* [*Preachers, Not Judges*]. Cairo, 1977.

Ibn `Abd al-Wahhab, Muhammad. *Kitab al-Tawhid* [*The Book of Monotheism*]. Raleigh: International Islamic Publishing House, 1998.

Keddie, Nikki R. *An Islamic Response to Imperialism: Political and Religious Writings of Sayyid Jamal al-Din "al-Afghani."* Berkeley: University of California Press, 1983.

Kepel, Gilles. *Muslim Extremism in Egypt: The Prophet and The Pharaoh.* Berkeley: University of California Press, 1985.

———. *Jihad: The Trail of Political Islam.* London: I. B. Tauris, 2006.

Knysh, Alexander. "A Clear and Present Danger: 'Wahhabism' as a Rhetorical Foil." *Die Welt des Islams* 44, (2004): 3–26.

Kostiner, Dayan, et al. *The Making of Saudi Arabia, 1916–1936: From Chieftaincy to Monarchical State.* London: Oxford University Press, 1993.

Lacey, Robert. *The Kingdom: Saudi Arabia and the House of Saud.* New York: Harcourt Brace Jovanovich, 1981.

Lawrence, T. E. *Seven Pillars of Wisdom.* New York: Doubleday, 1926.

Lia, Brynjar. *The Society of the Muslim Brothers in Egypt: The Rise of an Islamic Mass Movement.* Reading, U.K.: Ithaca Press, 1998.

Long, David E. *The Kingdom of Saudi Arabia.* Gainesville: University Press of Florida, 1997.

Maqdisi(al-), Abu Muhammad. *Kashf al-niqab `an Shari`at al-ghab [Unveiling the Law of the Jungle].* Published online at: http://tawhed.ws, 1998.

———. *Hadhihi `aqidatuna [This is Our Doctrine].* Published online at http://tawhed.ws, 2003.

———. *Al-Kawashif al-jaliyya fi kufr al-dawla al-Sa`udiyya, [The Shameful Actions Manifest in the Saudi State's Disbelief].* Published online at http://tawhed.ws, 2000.

Mamdani, Mahmood. *Good Muslim, Bad Muslim: America, the Cold War and the Roots of Terror.* New York: Random House, 2004.

McCants, William and Jarret Brachman. *The Militant Ideology Atlas.* West Point, NY: Combating Terrorism Center, U.S. Military Academy, 2005.

Mitchell, Richard. *The Society of Muslim Brothers.* New York: Oxford University Press, 1993.

National Commission on Terrorist Attacks upon the United States. *The 9/11 Commission Report.* New York: Norton, 2004.

Poston, Larry. *Islamic Da`wah in the West: Muslim Missionary Activity and the Dynamics of Conversion to Islam.* Oxford: Oxford University Press, 1992.

Rida, Muhammad Rashid, ed. *Majmu`at al-rasa'il wa'l-masa'il al-najdiyya [Compendium of Letters and Questions on the Najd].* Cairo: al-Manar Press, 1928.

———. *Al-Wahhabism wa'l-Hijaz [Wahhabism and the Hijaz].* Cairo: al-Manar Press, 1925.

Roy, Olivier. *The Failure of Political Islam.* Cambridge, MA: Harvard University Press, 1994.

Olivier, Roy. *Globalized Islam: The Search for a New Ummah.* New York: Columbia University Press, 2004.

Qutb, Sayyid. *Ma`alim fi'l-Tariq [Signposts].* Beirut and Cairo, 1980.

Safran, Nadav. *Saudi Arabia: The Ceaseless Quest for Security.* Ithaca, NY: Cornell University Press, 1988.

Sedgwick, Mark. "Saudi Sufis: Compromise in the Hijaz, 1925–1940." *Die Weld des Islams* 3 (1997): 349–368.

Steinberg, Guido. "Ecology, Knowledge and Trade in Central Arabia (Najd) during the Nineteenth and Early Twentieth Centuries," in Madawi al-Rasheed and Robert Vitalis eds. *Counter-Narratives: History, Contemporary Society and Politics in Saudi Arabia and Yemen.* New York: Palgrave Macmillan, 2004.

Wiktorowicz, Quintan. "Anatomy of the Salafi Movement." *Studies in Conflict and Terrorism* 2 (May 2006): 207–239.

———. "The New Global Threat: Transnational Salafis and Jihad." *Middle East Policy* 8 (December 2001): 18–38.

Wright, Lawrence. *The Looming Tower: Al-Qaida and the Road to 9/11.* New York: Knopf, 2006.

Zawahiri(al-), Ayman. Translated by Amjad M. Abu Nseir. *Fursan taht raya al-Nabi [Knights under the Prophet's Banner].* Casablanca: Dar al-Najaah al-Jadeedah, 2001.

Zayyat(al-), Montassir. Translated by Amjad M. Abu Nseir. *Ayman al-Zawahiri kama `araftahu [Ayman al-Zawahiri as I Knew Him].* Cairo: Dar Misr al-Mahroosa, 2002.

Index

About the Author

CHRIS HEFFELFINGER writes on trends in Islamist ideology and militancy. He is an FBI fellow at the Combating Terrorism Center at the United States Military Academy (West Point), where he created curriculum and taught counterterrorism courses for the FBI and Joint Terrorism Task Forces. He lives in Washington, DC.

9/26/11